Church:

Tracing Our Pilgrimage

Student Text

Carla E. Fritsch

Carol Masterson Waner

Reverend Donald M. Zuleger

Series Title   *Discipleship*

The Authors   Carla E. Fritsch, who earned her M.A. at John Carroll University, Cleveland, Ohio, is a religion teacher and theology department chairperson. She is the author of *Understanding Scripture* and the co-author of *Church History*, *Faith: Developing an Adult Spirituality*, and the nine booklet *Theological Perspectives* series.

Carol Masterson Waner, who teaches sacraments and church history at the secondary level, earned her B.A. at Saint Mary's College, Notre Dame, Indiana. She has taught religion for public school students in five different parishes in elementary, junior high, and high school programs.

Reverend Donald M. Zuleger, co-author of *Christian Scriptures* published in 1988 as a part of the *Centering Faith* Series, is a college professor and former director of a religion department at the secondary level. He earned master's degrees in divinity and theology at St. John's University, Collegeville, Minnesota.

The Publishing Team   Rose Schaffer, HM, M.A., President/Chief Executive Officer
Bernadette Vetter, HM, M.A., Vice President
Mary Anne Kovacs, M.A., Editor

Art Direction   Krina K. Walsh, B.S.I.D.

Cover and Illustrations   Reed Simon, B.F.A.

Nihil Obstat   Reverend Thomas W. Tifft, Ph.D., M. Div.
Censor Deputatis

Imprimatur   Most Reverend Anthony M. Pilla, DD
Bishop of Cleveland

January 27, 1995

The *nihil obstat* and *imprimatur* are official declarations that a book is free of doctrinal or moral error. No implication is contained therein that those who have granted the *nihil obstat* and *imprimatur* agree with the contents, opinions, or statements expressed.

Scripture texts are taken from *The New American Bible with Revised New Testament* copyright © 1986 by the Confraternity of Christian Doctrine, Washington, D.C. 20017 and are used with permission. All rights reserved.

ISBN 1–56077–350–2

List of credits on Acknowledgments page beginning on 192.

Contents

Part 2. From Preaching to Doctrine

iv

Part 3. From Monarchy to Reform

Part 4. From Luther to Trent

Part 5. From Modernism to the Modern Era

Introduction

Church:

Tracing Our Pilgrimage

You are cordially invited
to a guided tour of Catholicism
through the centuries.

Fun, Adventure, Discovery!
Pack your bags and travel with us.

What kind of tour, you ask?
Where am I going?

Believe it or not,
you are going on a pilgrimage.

What's a pilgrimage?

It's a journey, generally a long one,
to a special area, usually, a holy place.

x

Boring?

No! A pilgrimage can be fun and full of adventure. You visit new places, meet people, tell stories, and even gossip a bit. It can be like a holiday or vacation.

Pilgrims travel for a variety of reasons. Some go for religious reasons (*e.g.*, healing or penance); others for adventure; some are forced to go; a few join up along the way. An interesting aspect of pilgrimages is that you learn to depend on other people. Traveling together builds relationships and friendships. A pilgrimage can form a network of people, a support system of interaction. For individuals, it can lead to self-discovery.

But watch out! A pilgrimage can be dangerous. Along the way you might face robberies, storms, sickness, rebels to lead you astray, or personal crises, even despair. However, you will learn that good often rises out of struggles and difficulties.

Bright spots along the way may be found in hostels (resting places)—to take a break. Tour guides—holy dedicated people who can give new direction and inspiration to weary travelers—are another source. You may even meet some comic characters to lend spice to the journey.

This pilgrimage will be a journey through time as pilgrim people of God. It will reveal to you the Catholic Church's story that spans almost 2000 years. Come! Join us.

Part 1

From Jerusalem to Rome

But you will receive power when the holy Spirit comes upon you, and you will be my witnesses in Jerusalem, throughout Judea and Samaria, and to the ends of the earth.

—Acts 1:8

"See how these Christians love one another," remarked Justin Martyr, a pagan who later converted to Christianity. Unconditional love and simple, ethical lifestyle were the cornerstones of Christian communal living. People shared what they had with the needy, and everybody came out ahead. Daily, more and more people joined this new Christian religion. By the end of the first century, Christianity had spread to the center of the world as the people of the day knew it—the city of Rome itself. This was amazing for a group of people who had their start in a small town in Palestine!

How and why did Christianity spread so quickly? There were two basic reasons: the people and their message. The apostles, Paul, and others traveled throughout the Roman Empire spreading the Good News of Jesus' death and resurrection. The word *apostle* means one who is sent. Jesus commissioned the twelve to preach his message and baptize all people. The apostles took Jesus at his word. John went to Asia, Mark helped found the Church in Alexandria (Egypt), and tradition teaches that Thomas took Christianity into India.

The apostles' message was simple: God loved us so much that He sent His only Son, Jesus. Through the death and resurrection of Jesus, our sins are forgiven. Those who listened to this message found peace and hope for the future.

Two tour guides will help us through this first century of the Church's pilgrimage: Peter and Paul. Both traveled to Rome, but by separate paths. Both lost their lives because of their religious beliefs. Both are numbered among the great saints.

The apostles and Paul, by their witnessing, serve as an example to each of us. They faced hardship and had to wrestle with some very tough questions. They never compromised their values or beliefs. They "stood out" at a time when the whole world wanted to be "in." And believe it or not, eventually "standing out" was the "in" thing to do!

With the death of St. John the Evangelist, the youngest of the apostles, the period of the Church's journey with the companions of Jesus came to an end. No longer would Christians have the benefit of personal eyewitness stories of the words and actions of Jesus. Into the second century, the journey continued guided by disciples and students of Christ's apostles. Our new guides relied on the Holy Spirit to direct the way of the pilgrim Church.

Roman authorities demanded loyalty to their gods and the emperors. Failure to swear an oath of allegiance to the emperor and offer incense as sacrifice to the Roman gods meant death. Faithful pilgrims were martyred in gruesome public spectacles before cheering pagan crowds. But through it all, the Church grew until it became the dominant force in the Roman world.

Models of the Church

Directions: In *Models of the Church*, Avery Dulles outlines several different ways of understanding the Church. He stresses that the Church is a complex entity. Looking at only one or two aspects of the Church leads to an incomplete picture of the true nature of our faith. When viewed together, the models he describes help us understand the nature, function, and ministry of our Church. Read the following descriptions of the models.

The Church as a Mystical Communion

The mystical communion model of the Church emphasizes the kinds of relationships members of the Church have with one another. In much the same way as a family is united in love, members of the Church are united to one another through bonds of love and mutual trust. The interpersonal nature of our Christian fellowship is stressed so that all members of the community feel a part of the Church, looking to one another for companionship and friendship, as well as for strength and support.

Not all communities, however, are models for the Church. Church members have a relationship not only with one another, but also with God. This relationship is both individual and collective. Membership in the Christian community helps individuals nurture and support one another in faith. A sense of personal intimacy grows when people share with each other their own growth in relationship to God. The community as a whole is also called to a deeper faith in God. The community is responsible for sharing in the mission of bringing God's message of salvation to the world. God is present in the Christian community.

The images of the Body of Christ and the People of God illustrate the communal nature of the Church. These images emphasize our need to put God at the center of our Christian community and seek out new and different ways of experiencing God's presence in the world. It is specifically this religious aspect that distinguishes the Church as a mystical communion from other expressions of community found in our world.

If the Church were to be understood only as a community, however, it would lack the necessary organizational skills to insure that its work would continue. Without some sense of direction, a community loses the ability to function. The Church is no exception.

Christ meets us in the preaching as one crucified and risen. He meets us in the word of preaching and nowhere else. The faith of Easter is just this—the faith in the word of preaching.

—Rudolph Bultmann

3

The Church as an Institution

To accomplish the Christ's mission of establishing God's kingdom on earth, the Church must have an organized structure and a developed plan. This is the function of the institutional side of the Church. To unite people of all nations into a community of common conviction, commitment, and hope, the Church needs a stable, visible organization with responsible leaders and approved procedures.

Most people point to the roles assigned to the pope and bishops as examples of the function of the institutional Church. Certainly these people are part of it, but this model involves much more. The Church as an institution preserves the teachings of our faith from the time of Christ until now. Our scriptures, sacramental practices, and doctrines are all products of the institutional aspect of our community. The Church, when understood as an institution, provides us with a sense of corporate identity and membership. It enables us to understand who we are and why we do things the way we do them. The institutional nature of the Church lends a sense of meaning to our communal experience and provides us with a structure for the community to become stronger.

If the Church is understood only as an institution, however, people might get the mistaken impression that membership is reserved only for the most visible members of the organization, *i.e.*, the pope and bishops. Some people might see the institutional nature as an end in itself, rather than as a helpful structure to accomplish our work.

4

The Church as a Sacrament

Henri de Lubac, in his book *Catholicism* describes the Church this way:

If Christ is the sacrament of God, the Church is for us the sacrament of Christ; she represents him, in the full and ancient meaning of the term, she really makes him present. She not only carries on his work, but she is his very continuation, in a sense far more real than that in which it can be said that any human institution is its founder's continuation.[1]

As a sacrament, the church is called to signify in an historically tangible form the redeeming grace of Christ given to all people. Not only are the seven ritual sacraments part of this understanding; the Church itself is also recalled to make Christ present on earth. To do this the Church must continually strive to become more holy. The Church calls people to a sense of repentance and reconciliation just as it itself continually repents and seeks reconciliation. In a very real sense, the Church is called to become what it preaches—a means of encountering the risen Christ in present-day life.

If, however, the Church is understood only as a sacrament, then it runs the risk of being viewed superstitiously. Some people may see the Church as only a symbol or a type of spiritual filling-station where we go to get our weekly allotment of grace.

5

---

[1]H. de Lubac, *Catholicism*, (London: Burnes, Oates, and Washbourne, 1950), 29.

The Church as Herald

Before his ascension into Heaven, Jesus commissioned the Apostles to preach his message to all people on earth *(Matthew 28:16–20)*. When the Church acts as a herald, it concentrates on proclaiming the Good News (Gospel) of Jesus Christ to people of all lands and cultures. This understanding of Church is based upon the person of Jesus Christ, who is the Word-made-flesh *(John 1:1–14)*, and upon his message of salvation through faith in God. The Church has been entrusted with this message and is charged with sharing it boldly and with safeguarding its integrity. The Church's work in missionary activity, its evangelistic efforts, and its devotion to scripture study are all aspects of the understanding of Church.

When the Church is understood only as a herald, however, people may place so much emphasis on understanding scripture that they neglect their personal relationship with Jesus Christ. People may also run the risk of neglecting their duties to the community and adopt a "lone ranger" approach to their faith life. Without training, they may also misinterpret scripture.

The Church as Servant

The Church is called to follow the example of Jesus Christ, who came not only to proclaim the coming of God's kingdom, but also to offer his own life to bring it about. Jesus healed the sick and reached out to the brokenhearted; he reconciled people to God and to one another. The Church is called to this same type of service in our world. The Church must motivate people to use their power for service: to teach, help the sick and poor, visit the imprisoned. The Church calls us to work for justice for all people. In a world broken by violence and war, scarred by pollution and depletion of natural resources, and despairing because of a lack of hope for its people, the Church is called to remedy situations that need intervention. To this end, the Church sponsors outreach programs, soup kitchens, and clothing drives. It may also sponsor hospitals, schools and social advocacy services. All these efforts aim to ease the burden of suffering in the world.

Mother Teresa once said that without prayer her ministry would be nothing more than social work. If the Church is understood only as a servant, then some people might view the Church as a type of "social action committee." It is possible to divorce the action from the reason behind the action. We are called to remember that the Church serves people because Jesus did.

Each model of the Church has its own strengths and weaknesses. To understand the Church fully, we need all of the models together. Only then do we have a proper understanding of the scope of the Church's mission and the underlying reasons for that mission.

7

Character Sketches

Directions: Refer to the scripture passages listed; then read the character sketches below.

Peter: *(Read Matthew 16:18–19, Luke 22:31–34, Matthew 26:69–75.)* Your nickname is Rocky. On the outside you are strong and tough, but on the inside you are just a big marshmallow. Over and over again you professed your love for Jesus, yet, when the time came to prove it, you denied even knowing him. Some friend you turned out to be! You are always messing up things and then trying to make yourself look better than you really are. Deep down inside you are scared and very much ashamed. You would give anything to be able to undo your cowardice. After all, he did appoint you to be the leader of the Church. But what can you do? You're only a fisherman. There just has to be a way to keep the memory of Jesus alive.

John: *(Read John 13:23, John 19:25–27.)* You are the youngest of all the apostles, a teenager. Jesus was your closest and dearest friend. He was the first person really close to you to die. You were the only apostle at the crucifixion, and Jesus asked you to take care of his mother. You are devastated over Jesus' death, and the new responsibility of caring for Mary is resting heavily upon your shoulders. How will you help her through this grief when you are grieving yourself? There just has to be a way to keep the memory of Jesus alive.

Simon the Zealot: *(Read Luke 6:12–16, Acts 1:13–14.)* You are angry! You're mad at the Roman government for executing Jesus; at the Jewish authorities for handing him over; at Judas for turning him in and then killing himself. You are even mad at Jesus for not getting himself out of trouble when he had the chance. You had such dreams, such hopes for a new world free from this untolerable oppression. You can't believe that they have all gone down the drain. Well, they'll pay for this; they all will pay for it! There just has to be a way to keep the memory of Jesus alive.

Those who are led by the Holy Spirit have true ideas; that is why so many ignorant people are wiser than the learned. The Holy Spirit is light and strength.

—St. John Vianney

8

Thomas: *(Read John 20:24–29.)* You are skeptical. You are wondering if this whole Jesus thing was just a bad dream. Face facts: Jesus was here, then he was dead, then he was alive again; now he's gone for good. It seems too strange to be true. You don't know what to believe or whom to believe anymore. Was this whole thing just a game? Just a dirty trick? Will things ever be the same again? Were you a fool for becoming involved? Jesus was so different from anybody else you knew. He stood for something. There just has to be a way to keep the memory of Jesus alive.

Mary, Mother of Jesus: *(Read Luke 1:26–38, Luke 2:33–35, John 19:25–26.)* You are all alone in this world. Your parents are long dead, as is your husband; now your only son has been killed. It has not been an easy life. As an unwed mother there was much misunderstanding. Even Joseph had a hard time discerning God's will. God has a plan. You do not know what it is, you do not pretend to understand it, you do not even like it sometimes—but you do trust that somehow, someway God's will is done. No, the events of the last few days cannot be the end. There is indeed a way to keep your son's memory alive.

9

Peter's Speech

Directions: Read Peter's first speech in *Acts 2:14–41*, then answer the questions.

1. What enabled Peter to preach like this?

2. List the gifts Peter used in making this speech.

3. What was the result of Peter sharing his gifts with the rest of the people gathered for Pentecost?

4. What would have happened if Peter had not risked sharing his gifts?

5. What gifts do you possess? How can you share these gifts with the Church?

A vessel is known by the sound, whether it be cracked or not; so men are proved, by their speech, whether they be wise or foolish.

—Demosthenes

10

The Christian Community

Directions: Read the following description of the early Christian community; then answer the questions.

Love expressed in very specific ways was the hallmark of the first Christian communities. In a sense they were an early experiment in socialism. The followers of Jesus believed that no one should go without the necessities of life, especially not those most dependent on others, like widows and orphans. There were no social programs or life insurance benefits then!

The community provided for the needs of all by a system of voluntary poverty. Those who wished to do so sold everything they owned when they joined the community. The money from this sale was then laid at the feet of the apostles, who used it to provide food and other necessities for the poor. New members were encouraged, but not required, to do this.

In the Jerusalem community, there were Jews who spoke Greek, called Hellenists, and those who spoke Aramaic, the language that Jesus and most Jews of Palestine used. According to Acts of the Apostles, Hellenists began to complain that when daily rations were distributed their widows were receiving less than the widows of the Aramaic group.

The apostles were still instructing and baptizing the many new converts so it is not too difficult to imagine them throwing up their hands in exasperation at the pettiness of the fight. However, they were smart enough to recognize the danger to the community and acted immediately to deal with the problem of how to distribute food justly. The Book of Acts tells us that the apostles called an emergency meeting. The decision they made became the beginnings of an institutional Church.

> So the Twelve called together the community of the disciples and said, "It is not right for us to neglect the word of God to serve at table. Brothers, select from among you seven reputable men, filled with the Spirit and wisdom, whom we shall appoint to this task, whereas we shall devote ourselves to prayer and to the ministry of the word."
>
> —*Acts 6:2–4*

Community encourages, challenges, strengthens. Together, in faith, we can do more than anyone of us alone.

11

The men's function was to ensure the smooth daily running of the community. These assistants eventually became known as deacons. There is evidence that the office of deacon spread as the Church moved out of Palestine and into the larger Roman world. Women, too, became assistants or deaconesses. Paul (*Romans 16:1–2*) mentions Phoebe. She was called *diakonos* or minister, and Paul asked that the people of Rome help her in any way they could.

The deacons, then, made sure that arguments in the Christian community were settled in loving, just ways that protected the dignity of all the followers of Jesus.

1. In what sense was the early Christian community an experiment in socialism?

2. Describe the system of voluntary poverty practiced by the early Christians.

12

3. What two groups came into disagreement? What was the issue?

4. How did the apostles solve the problem?

5. What function did the deacons fulfill in the early Church?

Stephen's Journey in Faith

Directions: Read these scripture passages: *Acts 6:8–15, Acts 7:51–60, Acts 8:1–3.*

Each statement below represents a stepping-stone in Stephen's journey of faith. Read these statements. On the lines provided, rewrite them in the order in which they occurred. Then answer the question that follows.

Stephen is brought before the Sanhedrin to answer charges against him.

A persecution of the Christian community erupts in Jerusalem.

Stephen has a debate with some Jews who do not believe in Jesus.

Stephen is accused of blasphemy, the worst sin a Jew can commit since it insults God by making a creature equal to God.

"Lord Jesus, receive my spirit."

Stephen is buried by devout men.

Stephen preaches to the Jewish leaders and calls them "stiff-necked people" who murdered the Messiah sent by God.

Those killing Stephen leave their cloaks with a man named Saul, while they stone Stephen.

The leaders condemn Stephen to death by stoning, the traditional penalty for blasphemy.

Stephen sees a vision of Jesus at God's right hand.

"Lord, do not hold this sin against them."

13

Faith is necessary to victory.

—Hazlett

1. _____

   _____

2. _____

   _____

3. _____

   _____

4. _____

   _____

5. _____

   _____

6. _____

   _____

7. _____

   _____

8. _____

   _____

9. _____

   _____

10. _____

    _____

11. _____

    _____

Stephen is deliberately presented in Acts as a Christ-figure. What three parallels do you see between Stephen's martyrdom and the passion and death of Jesus?

14

Discovering St. Paul

Directions: Read the scripture passages listed below and answer the questions that follow.

> Acts 18:1–3
> Acts 21:37–40
> Acts 22:3–5,
> 2 Corinthians 11:24–29
> Philippians 3:5–6

1. Where was Paul born?

2. What was Paul's race?

3. What was Paul's religion?

4. What was Paul's tribe?

5. What languages did Paul speak?

6. What type of education did Paul receive?

7. What was Paul's position regarding the Jewish law?

8. How did Paul view the members of the Christian Church?

9. What was Paul's occupation or trade?

10. What kinds of hardships did Paul endure for Christ?

The Gospel falls upon man as God's own mighty Word, questioning him down to the bottom of his being, uprooting him from his securities and satisfactions, and therefore tearing clean asunder all the relations that keep him prisoner within his own ideals in order that he may be genuinely free for God and for his wonderful new work of grace in Jesus Christ.

—Karl Barth

15

The Call of St. Paul

Directions: St. Paul's conversion is described three times in the Acts of the Apostles. Read the following and identify in each the three elements of a call narrative.

1. *Acts 9:1–19*

    a. Call—

    b. Response—

    c. Mission—

2. *Acts 22:6–21*

    a. Call—

    b. Response—

    c. Mission—

3. *Acts 26:12–18*

    a. Call—

    b. Response—

    c. Mission—

I Am Chosen in Christ

Directions: Read the passages below, then answer the questions.

Blessed be the God and Father of our Lord Jesus Christ, who has blessed us in Christ with every spiritual blessing in the heavens, as he chose us in him, before the foundation of the world, to be holy and without blemish before him.

—*Ephesians 1:3–4*

In him we were also chosen, destined in accord with the purpose of the One who accomplishes all things according to the intention of his will, so that we might exist for the praise of his glory, we who first hoped in Christ.

—*Ephesians 1:11–12*

In what ways am I a holy person?

How does my life give praise to God?

When St. Paul was asked what the most important elements of life were, he said that they were the things you could not see. And the people in Rome said, "What are the things you can't see?" And he said, "Justice, peace, truth, service, humility, kindness, compassion, love." Those are the things that are most important, the things that never change.

—*Jimmy Carter*

17

Paul, the Traveler

Directions: Read the following description of Paul's missionary journeys.

Paul was a dynamic person who, after his conversion, worked tirelessly for the Gospel. In a sense he was the first pilgrim in the Church. He made three missionary journeys in the Roman world outside of Palestine. It is estimated that during his second journey alone he walked nine-hundred miles.

All his power and energy were directed to one end alone—making present the redeeming love of Jesus Christ. For this end Paul would endure everything, even death itself. The love of God expressed in his son, Jesus, was the only thing that mattered, and he burned with desire to reach everyone he encountered and tell them the good news. So he kept going, each journey taking longer and covering more territory. The words "impossible" or "too hard" simply were not part of his vocabulary.

After his conversion, probably around the year 34–35, he left Damascus. There is a time lapse of several years during which Paul was in Arabia, Tarsus (his hometown), again in Damascus, Jerusalem, and Antioch. In both Damascus and Jerusalem, he was met with fear and hatred from Jews and Christians alike. This is understandable when we realize that the Jews undoubtedly considered him a traitor and a betrayer of Jewish heritage. The Jews were so determined to kill Paul that his Christian friends had to lower him over the walls of Damascus in a large basket under the cover of darkness so he could escape detection and death. From there, he went to Jerusalem, but he ran into problems there, too. Many Christians suspected that Paul's conversion was a trick; to them Paul was like a double agent pretending to convert so he could report back to the Sanhedrin the identities and activities of the Christians. It took a long time for the Christian community to accept Paul. It also took time for Paul himself to absorb his experience, what it meant, and what he was supposed to do.

Around the year 46, Paul went on his first missionary trip with his friend, Barnabas, from Antioch. It was the shortest of his trips but set the pattern for the others. Paul never gave up his love for Judaism and the Jewish people; it was too much a part of his identity. Whenever he stopped at a city, he always went first to the Jewish synagogue to preach the good news.

Next, he began talking in the public places of the cities where gentiles gathered. Here, he sometimes had a more receptive audience. In the meantime, those who rejected his message would get a lynch mob organized, and Paul would be forced to flee the city just ahead of an angry crowd. Sometimes he did not escape from beatings or stonings; once he was left for dead.

Another pattern emerged from his first journey. Paul moved quickly into the centers of Asia Minor and then backtracked, checking on the progress of the small Christian communities he had founded earlier. This became the successful formula he used in his missionary activities: preaching, setting up a functioning community of believers, and then checking on them several weeks or months later on his way back home. Eventually, Paul also wrote letters when he could not visit a place. These became the famous Pauline epistles, an important part of the Christian Scriptures.

After returning from the first journey, Paul went to Jerusalem to report on his progress. Here he became a fierce spokesperson for the gentiles at the first major Church meeting, the Council of Jerusalem.

The second journey began shortly after the Council of Jerusalem, approximately 50 A.D., and lasted until about 53 A.D. On this trip, Paul, for the first time, visited Europe. The center of Christianity was progressively moving out of Jerusalem. Even in its first decades, the Church was a pilgrim Church on the move. It was on this journey that he wrote the first of his epistles, the letter to the Thessalonians.

Paul also made a third missionary journey, his longest in terms of time. This began in 53 and ended in 58 A.D. His fourth and last trip was not voluntary, since he went to Rome as a prisoner to go on trial before the emperor. There both Peter and Paul became victims of Emperor Nero's persecution. It is believed that Paul was beheaded and Peter died crucified upside down. Tradition indicates that Peter requested this because he did not feel worthy to die the same way Jesus did.

19

Paul's Life Journey

Dates	Events	Letters
35 A.D.	Conversion of Paul	
35–38 A.D.	Paul in "Arabia"	
38 A.D.	Paul visits Peter	
38–48 A.D.	Paul in Syria and Cilicia	
48–49 A.D.	Mission in Galatia (first missionary journey)	
49 or 50 A.D.	Council of Jerusalem	
50–52 A.D.	Mission in Philippi; Thessalonica, Berea, Athens, and Corinth (Second missionary journey)	1 Thessalonians
53–56 A.D.	Travel to Antioch, Ephesus, Galatia; Mission in Ephesus, Visit to Corinth Imprisonment in Ephesus (Third Missionary Journey)	Galatians 1 Corinthians 2 Corinthians Philippians Philemon
56 A.D.	Journey to Jerusalem	Romans
58 A.D.	Journey to Rome	
60 A.D.	Death of Paul	

20

Paul's Journeys

Use the following maps to trace Paul's steps on his missionary journeys.

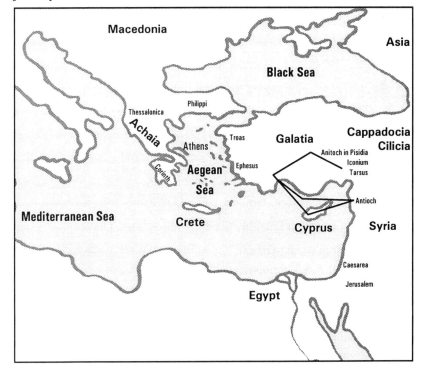

**First Missionary
Journey of Paul**

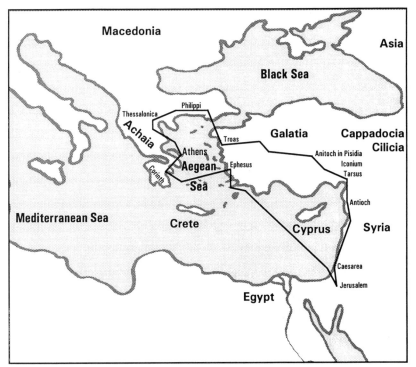

**Second Missionary
Journey of Paul**

Determine what modern-day countries are represented on the maps above.

Determine what modern-day countries are represented on the maps below.

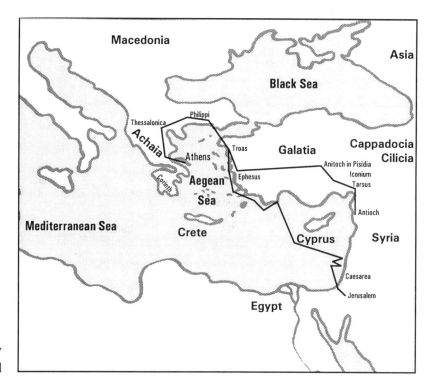

**Third Missionary
Journey of Paul**

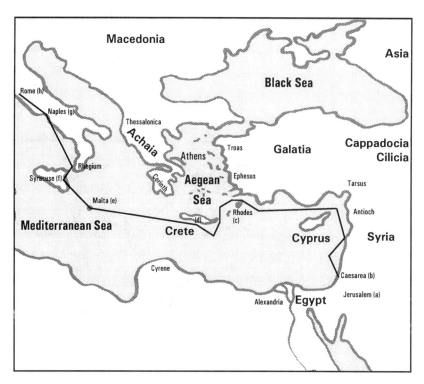

**Paul's
Journey to Rome**

From Jerusalem to Rome

Paul's Journey to Rome

Directions: Use a Bible to find a description of each event listed below. Skim to find the place where each event happened. On the line next to each statement below, fill in the letter of the appropriate location. A place may be used more than once; some places are not used. Places are lettered A–H. Refer to the map at the bottom of page 22.

_____ 1. Paul was arrested after being the central figure in a riot caused when the Jews accuse him of defiling the Temple *(Acts 21:27–36)*.

_____ 2. The Roman commander was fearful because he had allowed Paul, who was a Roman citizen, to be punished unlawfully *(Acts 22:22–29)*.

_____ 3. Paul was transferred there because the Jews were plotting to kill him *(Acts 23:12–23)*.

_____ 4. Felix, the governor, decided to put Paul on trial; he then changed his mind and just kept him in custody *(Acts 22:23–33 and 24:22–23)*.

_____ 5. Porcius Festus succeeded Felix and threatened to send Paul back to Jerusalem; Paul demanded his right as a Roman citizen to have his appeal heard by Caesar in Rome *(Acts 25:1–12)*.

_____ 6. Near this island, Paul's ship was caught in a severe storm and was eventually destroyed *(Acts 27:13–15)*.

_____ 7. Paul spent the winter months there *(Acts 28:1)*.

_____ 8. Paul was bitten by a poisonous snake while gathering firewood *(Acts 28:3–5)*.

_____ 9. After finding a new ship, Paul sailed to this place where he spent three days *(Acts 28:11–12)*.

_____ 10. Paul lived for two years under house arrest; this meant he was not in jail but was kept under guard *(Acts 28:16 and 30–31)*.

The Jerusalem Council

Directions: Read the description of the Council of Jerusalem.

Through the missionary activity of Peter and, more notably, Paul and Barnabas, the early Christian faith was brought to Greek-speaking communities far beyond Jerusalem. However, because gentiles favorably received the message about Jesus and through Paul's preaching accepted baptism in this new faith, a problem arose. Certain Jerusalem Christians, mostly converts from the Jewish religious party called the Pharisees, protested that gentiles should follow the Jewish ways before being baptized. This meant that they expected converts to obey the Mosaic laws, follow kosher dietary laws, observe the holy days of Jews and, if males, be circumcised. Paul and Barnabas had not demanded these practices of their gentile converts. This caused a big controversy in the early Church.

The Council of Jerusalem was called about 49 or 50 A.D. to deal with this controversy over the place of the gentile converts. At that time Christianity was still viewed as a part of the Jewish religion. It was only after this council that Christians would be viewed as a group separate and unique from Judaism. The council decided that gentile converts were not required to be circumcised. We find two accounts of this meeting in Acts 15 and Galatians 2.

The Council of Jerusalem set the pattern for all subsequent councils. This is important because it brought order, unity, organization, and stability to the Church at a crucial time when Christianity needed it.

The pattern of conciliary organization (the meeting of Church officials to decide Church issues) can be summarized as follows:

1. The Church recognizes a problem or issues affecting the whole Church.

2. A meeting is called with all the Church's leaders.

3. There is open discussion of all sides of the issues with prayers for guidance by the Holy Spirit.

4. The chief bishop (usually the pope, the Bishop of Rome) makes a decision acceptable to all sides.

5. The chief bishop makes a formal announcement of the council's conclusions.

This council also established the foundation for two other Church concepts that have contributed to unity:

Papal Primacy—The necessity of having a president or chief presider of the assembly who speaks in the name of the whole assembly concerning its results for the universal Church. In later centuries this position of leadership was filled by the Bishop of Rome.

Collegiality—A sharing in the decision-making process and authoritative positions taken by the leadership of Church. The bishops and pope, working together under the guidance of the Holy Spirit, chart the course for the future journey of the pilgrim people of God.

25

The Council Room

Directions: Compare the two Scriptural accounts of the Jerusalem Council. Read each passage; then answer the questions below.

Acts 15

1. Who went to Jerusalem?

2. What was the issue to be debated?

3. What group advocated the position contrary to Paul?

4. Who spoke on behalf of Paul?

5. What did he say?

6. Who made the final decision?

7. What was the decision?

Galatians 2:1–10

1. Who went to Jerusalem?

2. What was the issue to be debated?

3. What group advocated the position contrary to Paul?

4. Did Peter speak on behalf of Paul?

5. Who made the final decision?

6. What was the decision?

Church Councils at a Glance

Directions: Since the Council of Jerusalem there have been 21 Ecumenical Councils throughout Church history. Study the list below, then complete the exercise.

1. Nicea   325 A.D.

2. Constantinople I   381 A.D.

3. Ephesus   431 A.D.

4. Chalcedon   451 A.D.

5. Constantinople II   553 A.D.

6. Constantinople III   680–681 A.D.

7. Nicea II   787 A.D.

8. Constantinople IV   869–870 A.D.

9. Lateran I   1123 A.D.

10. Lateran II   1139 A.D.

11. Lateran III   1179 A.D.

12. Lateran IV   1215 A.D.

13. Lyons I   1245 A.D.

14. Lyons II   1274 A.D.

15. Vienne (France)   1311–1312 A.D.

16. Constance   1414–1418 A.D.

17. Florence   1431–1445 A.D.

18. Lateran V   1512–1517 A.D.

19. Trent   1545–1563 A.D.

20. Vatican   1869–1870 A.D.

21. Vatican II   1962–1965 A.D.

1. Research and define the term *ecumenical* as it applies to a Church council.

2. Pick any one council. Prepare a report to include information about the pope during the council, the main issues facing the council, and the impact of the council's decision upon the Church as a whole.

3. Imagine where and when the next Church council might convene. Describe in writing what issues that council might be called upon to address.

The Roman Persecutions

Directions: Read the following information about Rome's persecution of the early Christians and answer the questions. The following Roman emperors were responsible for persecutions against the Christian Church:

Nero (54–68) Nero started the persecutions by blaming Christians for the Fire of Rome in 64 A.D.

Domitian (81–96) Domitian considered himself to be divine and required all Roman citizens to offer sacrifice to his image. When Christians refused, they were arrested and jailed.

Hadrian (117–138) Hadrian continued the local persecutions against Christians, but he also made it more difficult to martyr the believers.

Marcus Aurelius (161–181) Marcus Aurelius blamed several natural disasters on Christians. He approved the massacre of the Christian community in Gaul (France).

Septimius Severus (202–211) Septimius Severus prohibited conversion to Christianity and launched a severe persecution in North Africa.

Decius (249–251) Decius launched the first large-scale persecution of the Christian community. All were required to present certificates proving their sacrifice to the pagan gods. Christian property was confiscated, jobs were sacrificed, and many people lost their lives.

Valerian (257–260) Valerian resumed the Decian persecution after a brief respite.

Diocletian (284–305) Diocletian launched the most severe and bloody persecution of the Christian community. Christians were prohibited from meeting; they were arrested, tortured, and killed.

Galerius (305–311) Galerius continued Diocletian's persecution and killed many who refused to sacrifice to his name.

> ... if the sky does not move or the earth does, if there is famine, if there is plague, the cry is at once: "The Christians to the lion!"
>
> —Tertullian

29

How did citizens of the Roman Empire react to the persecutions? This passage from the writings of Tacitus offers some insight:

To kill the rumors, Nero charged and tortured some people hated for their evil practices—the group popularly knows as 'Christians.' The founder of this sect, Christ, had been put to death by the governor of Judea, Pontius Pilate, when Tiberius was Emperor. Their deadly superstition had been suppressed temporarily, but was beginning to spring up again—not now just in Judea but even in Rome itself where all kinds of sordid and shameful activities are attracted and catch on.

First those who confessed to being Christians were arrested. Then, on information obtained from them, hundreds were convicted, more for their antisocial beliefs than for fire-raising. In their deaths they were made a mockery. They were covered in the skins of wild animals, torn to death by dogs, crucified or set on fire—so that when darkness fell they burned like torches in the night. Nero opened up his own gardens for this spectacle and gave a show in the arena, where he mixed with the crowd, or stood dressed as a charioteer on a chariot. As a result, although they were guilty of being Christians and deserved death, people began to feel sorry for them. For they realized that they were being massacred not for the public good but to satisfy one man's mania.

—*Tacitus,* Annals *15.44*

Can you think of other instances when people have been made scapegoats for the problems and misfortunes of others?

The Letter to Diognetus

Directions: This anonymous letter, dating from the second century, describes the extraordinary witness of the Christian faith. Read it carefully; then reflect on the question at the end.

For Christians are not differentiated from other people by country, language or customs; you see, they do not live in cities of their own, or speak some strange dialect, or have some peculiar lifestyle.

This teaching of theirs has not been contrived by the invention and speculation of inquisitive men; nor are they propagating mere human teaching as some people do. They live in both Greek and foreign cities, wherever chance has put them. They follow local customs in clothing, food and other aspects of life. But at the same time, they demonstrate to us the wonderful and certainly unusual form of their own citizenship.

They live in their own native lands, but as aliens; as citizens, they share all things with others; but like aliens, suffer all things. Every foreign country is to them as their native country, and every native land as a foreign country.

They marry and have children just like everyone else; but they do not kill unwanted babies. They offer a shared table, but not a shared bed. They are at present "in the flesh" but they do not live "according to the flesh." They are passing their days on earth, but are citizens of heaven. They obey the appointed laws, and go beyond the laws in their own lives.

They love everyone, but are persecuted by all. They are unknown and condemned; they are put to death and gain life. They are poor and yet make many rich. They are short of everything and yet have plenty of all things. They are dishonored and yet gain glory through dishonor.

Their names are blackened and yet they are cleared. They are mocked and bless in return. They are treated outrageously and behave respectfully to others. When they do good, they are punished as evil-doers; when punished, they rejoice as if being given new life. They are attacked by Jews as aliens, and are persecuted by Greeks; yet those who hate them cannot give any reason for their hostility.

To put it simply—the soul is to the body as Christians are to the world. The soul is spread through all parts of the body and Christians through all the cities of the world. The soul is in the body but is not of the body; Christians are in the world but not of the world.[1]

Does this letter also describe your own experience of Christianity? Explain what is necessary to recapture the depth of spirit the early Christians possessed.

[1]Tim Dowley, ed., *Eerdmans' Handbook to the History of Christianity* (Oxford, England: Lion Publishing, 1977), 69.

31

Early Christian Martyrs

Directions: Beginning in 64 A.D. in Rome under Nero, Christians were systematically hunted down, arrested, tortured, and killed because of their belief in Jesus as the Christ. For almost 250 years (64–310 A.D.) these persecutions went on all over the Roman Empire under ten different Roman emperors. During this time period, over one-million Christians were put to death. The worst persecution occurred under Emperor Diocletian.

Research these early martyrs. Explain how they died, when the Church celebrates their feasts, and how they are entitled as patrons.

1. St. Agnes

2. St. Apollonia

3. St. Barbara

4. St. Blaise

5. St. Cecilia

6. St. Lawrence

7. St. Lucy

8. Sts. Perpetua and Felicity

9. St. Sebastian

10. St. Tarcisius

. . . saints, in order to reach sanctity, have had to follow the path which God has made peculiarly theirs.

—Abbé de Tourville

32

From Jerusalem to Rome

Apostolic Fathers

Directions: Read the following information about the Apostolic Fathers.

The writings of the Apostolic Fathers provide a rich insight into how the Christian faith survived after the death of the apostles. Because many of these writers were disciples or contemporaries of the apostles, they were called Apostolic Fathers. Some of them use an apologetic style: their writings are polemics or justifications defending the Christian faith. The Apostolic Fathers have left a rich foundation and heritage of faith for all Christians.

St. Clement of Rome was the third successor to St. Peter (after Linus and Anacletus). He served as Bishop of Rome from 88–97 A.D. His name is linked to a letter addressed to the Church at Corinth, which sheds light on how the Church worked soon after the Age of the Apostles. This letter is probably the earliest surviving Christian text outside of the Christian Testament.

St. Clement used the letter to illustrate the division of roles and responsibilities in the Church. He described bishops (*episkopoi*) as overseers of the Church community, responsible to safeguard the integrity of the Christian message and preside at the eucharistic assembly. Elders (*presbyteroi*) were community leaders who helped guide the community's spiritual growth. Deacons (*diakonoi*) were to tend to the temporal needs of the community through the collection and distribution of charitable donations. The letter also describes a simple understanding of apostolic succession, the unbroken line of authority traced through Peter and his legitimate successors.

St. Ignatius of Antioch (50–107 A.D.) succeeded St. Peter as bishop of Antioch and was a disciple of the apostle John. He was the first person to use the term *catholic* (universal) to describe the Church. Ignatius stressed the necessity for unity within the church. He saw the role of bishop as vital to maintaining that unity. His letters call for each community to have its own bishop and for that bishop to look to Christ as an example of true leadership.

Ignatius also stressed the need for the community to come together for prayer and worship, and especially to celebrate Eucharist. So great was his devotion to the Eucharist that, on his way to face the lions at his martyrdom, he said, "I am (God's) wheat, ground fine by the lion's teeth, to be made purest bread for Christ."

If you do not hope, you will not find what is beyond your hopes.

—St. Clement of Alexandria

33

Organization of the Church

Directions: St. Clement's letter describes roles and functions within the early Church. Today we have a similar structure. Examine the chart below, and answer the questions that follow. You may need to do some research to answer all of the questions.

Pope/Bishop of Rome

West	East
Province (archbishop)	**Patriarchate** (patriarch)
Diocese (bishop) (auxiliary bishop)	**Eparchy** (bishop)
Deanery (dean)	**Parish** (pastor) (associate pastor) (deacon)
Parish (pastor) (associate pastor) (deacon) (parish council president)	

1. Who is the current Bishop of Rome?

2. In what province do you live?

3. Who is the archbishop there?

4. In what diocese do you live?

5. Who is the bishop there?

6. Who is (are) the auxiliary bishop(s)?

7. In what parish do you live? Do you attend this parish? If not, where do you attend?

8. What is the name of your pastor?

9. What is (are) the name(s) of the associate pastor(s)?

10. Does your parish have a deacon? What is his name?

11. What is the name of your parish council president?

12. Is anyone your age a member of your parish council?

The
life of a
conscientious
clergyman
is not
easy.

—Samuel
Johnson

34

From Jerusalem to Rome

Peter's Journey in Faith

Part A

Directions: Read and reflect on the passages below in the order listed. Be prepared to share your reflections with the class.

1. *John 1:40–42*   We have found the Messiah!

2. *Luke 5:1–11*   Leave me, Lord. I am a sinful man.

3. *Mark 8:27–30*   You are the Messiah.

4. *Mark 8:31–33*   Get behind me, Satan.

5. *Matthew 18:21–22* How many times must I forgive?

6. *John 6:66–69*   Lord, to whom shall we go?

7. *Matthew 14:26–33* Lord, save me!

8. *Mark 5:35–37*   He took Peter, James and John.

9. *Mark 9:2–7*   Lord, it is good for us to be here!

10. *John 13:3–9*   You'll never wash my feet.

11. *John 13:21–24*   Peter motioned to him to ask.

12. *Luke 22:31–34*   I am prepared to go to prison.

13. *Mark 14:31*   I will not deny you.

14. *Matthew 26:37–41* Asleep, Simon?

15. *Matthew 26:69–75* I do not know the man!

16. *John 20:1–9*   Peter started out for the tomb.

17. *John 21:3–7*   Peter jumped into the water.

18. *John 21:15–19*   Do you love me?

35

Part B

Directions: Answer the questions below.

1. How did Peter first come to follow Jesus?

2. Was Peter the model disciple? Cite examples to support your answer.

3. What do the scriptures reveal about the type of person Peter was?

4. Why do you think Peter was made the leader of the church community?

5. What lessons does Peter's journey in faith teach us about our role in the church?

36

A Conversion Creates a Crisis

Directions: Read the following information about the conversion of Constantine.

The last of the Roman persecution was also the most bloody. It was begun by Diocletian around the year 303. The Empire had many problems, and Christians became a handy scapegoat. There may also have been a tinge of jealousy by the conservatives of the time who saw the vitality and growth of Christianity as a signal that old traditions were breaking down.

Certainly, the Empire required some major repair. A huge 6,000–mile frontier needed watching. The ability of the Roman government to control the borders was lessening, while the power of the army defending them was growing.

As a solution to the problem, Diocletian, a general, divided the Empire in two. He moved to the eastern part of the empire, where most of the difficulties were. He then assigned another man to stay in Rome to govern the West. He also allowed himself to be persuaded that persecuting the Christians would aid his cause.

Eventually, Diocletian was forced to resign because even his allies became disgusted with the bloodbath he unleashed. His government quickly disintegrated as rivals fought for power. Into this boiling cauldron stepped Constantine, who was to have a profound effect on the Church.

His influence began with a religious experience. It occurred the day before the Battle of the Milvian Bridge in 312. This was fought just north of Rome to determine who would win Rome and control the empire in the West. Constantine, not a Christian, was told in a vision to use a Christian symbol during the upcoming battle. He did, and he won. As a result, he became the first Christian emperor. He radically changed both the Church of his time and the Church of the future.

The Edict of Milan in 313 granted freedom of religion to everyone in the empire, with Christians getting special mention. It also ordered that all property which had been taken from the Church be returned.

Before God can deliver us from ourselves, we must undeceive ourselves.

—Augustine

37

In 324 Constantine defeated the eastern ruler and reunited the empire. This did not mean, though, that he wanted the old Rome to return. He had grander ideas than that. He decided to celebrate his victory by creating a "New Rome" further east. He chose Byzantium, a Greek city which straddled Europe and Asia, because of its location between the Black Sea and the Mediterranean Sea. Byzantium died, and Constantinople rose from its dust. Constantine's goal was to maintain unity at all costs. He did not know that his beautiful, powerful capital would later become a rival to Rome, resulting in suspicion, misunderstanding, disunity, and sometimes open warfare.

From Constantinople new laws and programs continued to flow, many giving the Christian Church increased security. In fact, Constantine perceived the Church as a means to achieve the unity so important to him. He decreed that clergymen were not required to give military service or pay certain taxes; bishops were given honors and allowed sometimes to act as judges. New social legislation was based on Christian morality. Punishments were made more humane, married men were forbidden to go to prostitutes, and children were given new protections. He also ordered the building of many new churches and provided public money. Imagine the reaction of some of the older bishops who had lived through Diocletian's bloodbath: they went in one lifetime from being considered traitors to being honored and protected by the empire!

Why was this a crisis for the Church? Christians began to influence society in positive ways. Many new converts entered, and new churches to accommodate them were built. Monasticism developed rapidly. Peace allowed a persecuted church to become a secure Church.

On the other hand, some say Constantine's rule was one of the worst things that ever happened to the Church. Becoming a Christian became easy and required little commitment or risk. People converted for social, upwardly mobile reasons instead of God-centered ones. Some bishops were great politicians but terrible pastors. The State now began to influence the Church to the point that political leaders, like Constantine and those who followed, made decisions about Church matters. This caused anxieties and potential dangers to the Church and the Gospel.

The Conversion of Constantine

Directions: The Christogram is an early form of the cross. It is made from the first two Greek letters in the word Christ; it looks like an X superimposed over a P. Below is a drawing of the battle standard which Constantine ordered made after his conversion. On the left side of the standard, list the positive results Constantine's rule accomplished for the Church; on the right side, list the negative results.

Positive   Negative

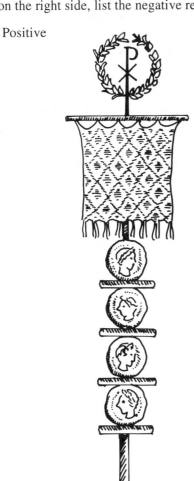

The Labarum of Constantine[1]

What do you think? Was Constantine's effect on the Church more positive or more negative? Why?

39

[1]Carl Van Treeck and Aloysius Croft, M.A., *Symbols in the Church* (Milwaukee: Bruce Publishing Co., 1936), 21.

From Jerusalem to Rome

Exercise 23

Comparing Conversions

Directions: *The Life of Constantine* was a fourth-century book written by Eusebius, a friend of the emperor. In it, he describes the experience which led to Constantine's conversion. Read Eusebius' account and answer the question given.

Around noontime, when the day was already beginning to decline, he saw before him in the sky the sign of a cross of light. He said it was above the sun and it bore the inscription, "Conquer with this." The vision astounded him, as it astounded the whole army which was with him on this expedition and which also beheld the miraculous event.

He said he became disturbed. What could the vision mean? He continued to ponder and to give great thought to the question, and night came on him suddenly. When he was asleep, the Christ of God appeared in the sky. He ordered Constantine to make a replica of this sign which he had witnessed in the sky, and he was to use it as a protection during his encounters with the enemy.[1]

Compare Constantine's conversion to Peter's experience with Cornelius (*Acts 10*) and to Paul's conversion on the road to Damascus (*Acts 9:1–9*). Include specific likenesses and differences.

40

[1]Colm Luibheid, ed., trans., *The Essential Eusebius* (New York: New American Library, 1966), 184–185.

Part 2

From Preaching to Doctrine

For the time will come when people will not tolerate sound doctrine but, following their own desires and insatiable curiosity, will accumulate teachers and will stop listening to the truth and will be diverted to myths.

—2 Timothy 4:3–4

On the pilgrimage, false guides stepped forward to lead the people of God along wayward paths. They were recognized eventually, but only after leading many people astray. True guides emerged too, using the Christian Scriptures left behind by Matthew, Mark, Luke, John, Peter, Paul, and others. These new guides preached and aided future pilgrims on their journey of fidelity. Through it all, the church grew in faith, learned what it meant to live a Christian lifestyle, and began to define its most central beliefs. The focus of Christian preaching shifted from Jesus *as* the message to the *meaning of* Jesus' message. Eventually, the Christian Church surfaced an identifiable creed (system of belief), code (system of practices and standards of behavior), and cult (system of worship and prayer).

Heresies at a Glance

Directions: Use the chart below to study the challenges heresies posed to the growing Church.

Heresy and Teaching	Council	Church Father	Catholic Doctrine
Gnosticism: salvation comes through secret knowledge given only to gnostics. Spirit is good; matter is evil.			Salvation is open to all.
Donatism: sacraments are valid only when performed by a holy and worthy priest. Only donatists belong to the true Church.	Arles (314)	St. Augustine	Sacraments convey grace independent of the holiness of the priest.
Novatianism: serious sin cannot be forgiven. Only holy people can be part of the Church.	Nicea (325)	St. Augustine	All sins can be forgiven.
Arianism: Jesus is a lesser god, a being created by God. Jesus does not possess by nature any divine qualities. The Father adopted him as son.	Nicea (325) Constantinople (381)	St. Athanasius St. Basil St. Gregory Nazianzan St. Ambrose St. Augustine	Jesus has the same nature as God. Nicene Creed
Nestorianism: Jesus and God share common wills, not natures. Mary is not the mother of God; she is the mother of Jesus as the Christ.	Ephesus (431)	St. Cyril of Alexandria Pope Clement	There are TWO natures in Christ; fully divine/fully human. Mary is the Mother of God.
Monophysitism: Jesus is God and only appeared to be human.	Chalcedon (451) II Constantinople (681)	Pope Leo I	Jesus Christ is one person with two natures.
Pelagianism: we can earn our own salvation; we do not need God's gift of grace.	Carthage (417)	Pope Innocent I St. Augustine	Doctrine of original sin One needs divine grace for salvation.
Manichaeism: The world is evil; we can be freed from it through ascetic discipline; reincarnation.		St. Augustine	The true task of the Church is to act as a sign of God's saving love for the world.
Iconoclasm: the veneration of religious images and icons is idolatrous and a violation of the first commandment.	II Nicea (726)	Pope Adrian I	The use of holy images is good and useful for devotion. It shows respect for God, Mary, and the saints who are represented by the icons.

43

From Preaching to Doctrine

Heresies, Councils, and Theologians

Directions: Based on the clues provided, determine which heresy, council, or theologian is described.

1. _ _ _ _ _ _ _ _ _ _ _ E

2. _ _ _ A _ _ _ _ _ _ _

3. _ R _ _ _ _ _ _

4. L _ _

5. _ _ _ _ _ _ Y _ _ _ _ _ _

6. C _ _ _ _ _ _ _

7. _ _ H _ _ _ _ _

8. _ U _ _ _ _ _ _ _ _

9. _ R _ _ _ _

10. _ _ _ _ C _ _ _ _ _ _ _

11. _ _ H _ _ _ _ _ _ _

12. _ H _ _ _ _ _ _ _

13. _ E _ _ _ _ _ _ _ _ _ _ _

14. _ _ R _ _ _ _

15. _ E _ _ _ _ _ _ _ _ _

16. _ _ _ _ _ _ S _

17. I _ _ _ _ _ _ _ _ _ _

18. _ _ _ E _

19. _ _ _ S _ _ _ _ _ _

Clues:

1. Two councils were held in this city (381 and 681). Both councils addressed the divine nature of Jesus.

2. This heresy taught that only holy people could be part of the Church.

3. This heresy taught that Jesus was the adopted son of God.

4. This pope fought against Monophysitism.

5. This heresy overemphasized the divine nature of Jesus.

6. This pope declared that Mary was the Mother of God.

7. This council emphasized that Jesus was both human and divine.

8. This theologian fought against Donatism, Novatianism, Arianism, Pelagianism, and Manichaeism.

9. This council was called to combat Donatism.

10. This heresy taught reincarnation.

11. This Father of the Church fought against Arianism with Saints Basil, Gregory, Ambrose, and Augustine.

12. This council was one of two which addressed the problem of Monophysitism.

13. This heresy stated that Jesus and God were not of the same nature.

14. This pope taught that holy images or icons were useful in devotion.

15. This heresy denied the need for grace.

16. This heresy taught that the validity of sacraments depended on the holiness of the priest.

17. This heresy was based on a strict interpretation of the first commandment.

18. This council helped to formulate the creed we recite today at mass.

19. This heresy taught that knowledge equals salvation.

45

The Nicene Creed

Directions: Read the creed carefully. Answer the questions that follow.

We believe in one God
the Father, the Almighty
maker of heaven and earth,
of all that is seen and unseen.

We believe in one Lord, Jesus Christ,
the only Son of God,
eternally begotten of the Father,
God from God, light from light
true God from true God,
begotten, not made, one in being with the Father.
Through him all things were made.
For us, and for our salvation
he came down from heaven:
by the power of the Holy Spirit
he was born of the Virgin Mary and became man.
For our sake he was crucified under Pontius Pilate;
he suffered, died, and was buried.
On the third day he rose again
in fulfillment of the Scriptures.
He ascended into heaven
and is seated at the right hand of the Father.
He will come again in glory to judge the living
and the dead,
and his kingdom will have no end.

We believe in the Holy Spirit, the Lord the giver of life,
who proceeds from the Father and the Son.
With the Father and the Son he is worshipped and glorified.
He has spoken through the prophets.
We believe in one, holy, catholic, and apostolic Church.
We acknowledge one baptism for the forgiveness of sins.
We look for the resurrection of the dead
and the life of the world to come. Amen.

1. Why is the section about Jesus so much longer than the other two sections?

2. Underline all statements in this creed that contradict heresies. What heresies are denied?

Faith Statements

Directions: Read the following creeds carefully. Be prepared to share your reflections with the class.

Monika Hellwig's Creed

We believe that happiness awaits humankind and that our existence is not absurd. We believe that all human longings can be fulfilled beyond imagining and that hope is not in vain.

We believe that we come into existence by love and that our lives can become wholly meaningful by love. We believe that all are joined in one destiny and that we are all responsible for one another.

We believe that peace, justice and freedom from want are God's gift to all but they must be freely received. We believe that no human being is forgotten by God and that no one can be unimportant to us.

We believe it because of Jesus who has reflected to us the fidelity of the Father. We believe it because of the sublime simplicity of his preaching and of his life.

We believe it because of the luminous conviction and singleness of purpose which he faced death. We believe it because the Father has raised him up as a sign of hope and challenge to all humanity that shall one day be gloriously fulfilled.

We believe it because of the Spirit that is among the followers of Jesus to this day. We believe it because of the assembling of the nations of unity and hope that has begun, and must yet be completed.

We believe it because we share in the celebration of the mysteries in which we are transformed. We believe it because we expect to share in the fulfillment of all the promises in a world yet to come. Let it be so: this is our commitment.[1]

47

[1]Monika Hellwig, *The Christian Creeds*, (Dayton: Pflaum/Standard Publishing, 1973), 96.

Creed of Edward Schillebeeckx

48

> The one thing that matters is that we always say yes to God whenever we experience him.
>
> —*Julian of Norwich*

I believe in God, the Father; the omnipotence of love. He is the Creator of heaven and earth; this whole universe, with all its mysteries; this earth on which we live, and the stars to which we travel. He knows us from eternity, he never forgets that we are made of the dust of the earth and that one day we shall return again to it as dust.

I believe in Jesus Christ, the only-beloved son of God. For love of all of us, he has willed to share our history, our existence with us. I believe that God also wanted to be our God in a human way.

He has dwelt as man among us, a light in the darkness. But the darkness did not overcome him. We nailed him to the cross. And he died and was buried. But he trusted in God's final word, and is risen, once and for all; he said that he would prepare a place for us, in his Father's house, where he now dwells.

I believe in the Holy Spirit, who is the Lord and gives life. And for the prophets among us, he is language, power, and fire. I believe that together we are all on a journey, pilgrims, called and gathered together, to be God's holy people, for I confess freedom from evil, the task of bringing justice and the courage to love.

I believe in eternal life, in love that is stronger than death, in a new heaven and a new earth. And I believe that I may hope for a life with God and with one another for all eternity: Glory for God and peace for men.[2]

[2]Edward Schillebeeckx, *Christ: The Experience of Jesus as Lord*, (N.Y.: Crossroads, 1980), 847.

From Preaching to Doctrine

We believe in the one High God, who out of love created the beautiful world and everything good in it. He created man and wanted man to be happy in the world. God loves the world and every nation and tribe on the earth. We have known this High God in the darkness, and now we know him in the light. God promised in the book of his word, the Bible, that he would save the world and all the nations and tribes.

We believe that God made good his promise by sending his son, Jesus Christ, a man in the flesh, a Jew by tribe, born poor in a little village, who left his home and was always on safari doing good, curing people by the power of God, teaching about God and man, showing that the meaning of religion is love. He was rejected by his people, tortured and nailed hands and feet to a cross and died. He lay buried in the grave, but the hyeneas did not touch him, and on the third day he rose from the grave. He ascended to the skies. He is the Lord.

We believe that all our sins are forgiven through him. All who have faith in him must be sorry for their sins, be baptized in the Holy Spirit of God, live the rules of love and share the bread together in love, to announce the good news to others until Jesus comes again. We are waiting for him. He is alive. He lives. This we believe. Amen.[3]

[3]Vincent J. Donovan, *Christianity Rediscovered,* (Notre Dame: Fides-Claretian, 1978), 200.

Theology Develops

> *From the Christian point of view faith belongs to the existential; God did not appear in the character of a professor who has some doctrines which must first be believed and then understood.*
>
> —Soren Kierkegaard

Directions: Read each of the passages listed below. Answer the questions that follow.

1. The Preaching of Jesus

   a. *Matthew 4:23*
      Summary:

   b. *Mark 1:14–15*
      Summary:

   c. *Luke 1:22–34*
      Summary:

   d. In general, what did Jesus preach?

2. The Preaching of the Apostles

   a. *Acts 3:11–26*
      Summary:

   b. *1 Corinthians 1:18–25*
      Summary:

   c. *Philippians 2:5–11*
      Summary:

   d. In general, what did the Apostles preach?

3. The Preaching of the Apostolic Fathers

a. The Church spreads out over the whole world to the
   uttermost ends of the earth. From the apostles and their
   disciples she received the faith: in the one God, the Almighty
   Father, Creator of Heaven and earth, the sea, and all that is
   in them; in the one Christ [Messiah] Jesus, the Son of God,
   who for our salvation took on flesh; and in the Holy Spirit
   who through the prophets proclaimed God's plan of salvation
   and the twofold coming of the Lord, His birth from a virgin,
   His suffering, His resurrection from the dead, the bodily
   ascension into Heaven of our beloved Lord, the Christ
   [Messiah] Jesus, and His future coming from the Heavens
   in the glory of the Father "to make all things new" and to
   raise up anew all flesh of the whole human race in order
   to execute judgment justly on all.

   Irenaeus, *Against Heresies* I.9.4; IV. 33; I.10.1.

   Summary:

b. I have heard certain people say, "What I cannot find in the
   ancient records, I do not believe in the Gospel." And when I
   said to them, "It is written!" they answered me, "That is just the
   question." But my records are Jesus Christ. The unassailable
   records are His Cross, His death, His resurrection, and the faith
   bestowed through Him; by these I want to be justified through
   your prayers.

       The priests, too, were good, but better is the High Priest
   to whom alone is entrusted the Holy of Holies, to whom alone
   are entrusted the hidden things of God. He is the Door to the
   Father through which alone enter Abraham and Isaac and
   Jacob and the prophets, and the apostles and the Church.
   All this comes together in the unity of God. One thing,
   however, makes the Gospel stand out above all: the advent
   of the Healing Savior, our Lord Jesus Christ, His suffering,
   and His resurrection. Certainly, the beloved prophets pointed
   to Him in their prophecies, but the Gospel is the consummation
   of incorruption. All these together are good if you have faith
   through love.

   Ignatius, *Letter to the Philadelphians* 8–9.

   Summary:

c. Let us therefore hold unceasingly to our expectation, to the guarantee of our future righteousness. This is Jesus Christ, who carried our sins on His own body up to the Tree, who committed no sin. No guile could be found in His words, but He suffered everything for our sake so that we should live in Him. Therefore let us become imitators of His patience, and if we must suffer for the sake of His name, then let us glorify Him. In this He gave us an example in His own person, and in this we believed.

Polycarp, *Letter to the Philippians*. Attested to by Irenaeus, *Against Heresies* III.3.4; Eusebius, III.36.13–15.[1]

Summary:

In general, what do the Apostolic Fathers preach?

5 2

[1]Eberhard Arnold, *The Early Christians* (Ripton, N.Y.: Plough Publishing House, 1972) 130, 163, 205.

From Preaching to Doctrine

4. Preaching of the Greek Fathers

    a. The kind of doctrines which are believed in plain terms through the apostolic teaching are the following:

        First, that God is one, who created and set in order all things, and who, when nothing existed, caused the universe to be. He is God from the first creation and foundation of the world, the God of all righteous men, of Adam, Abel, Seth, Enos, Enoch, Noah, Shem, Abraham, Isaac, Jacob, of the twelve patriarchs, of Moses and the prophets. This God, in these last days, according to the previous announcements made through his prophets, sent the Lord Jesus Christ, first for the purpose of calling Israel, and secondly, after the unbelief of the people of Israel, of calling the Gentiles also. This just and good God, the Father of our Lord Jesus Christ, himself gave the law, the prophets and the gospels, and he is God both of the apostles and also of the Old and New Testaments.

        Then again: Christ Jesus, he who came to earth was begotten of the Father before every created thing. And after he had ministered to the Father in the foundation of all things, for *all things* were *made through him*, in these last times he emptied himself and was made man, was made flesh, although he was God; and being made man, he still remained what he was, namely, God. He took to himself a body like our body, differing in this alone, that it was born of a virgin and of the Holy Spirit. And this Jesus Christ was born and suffered in truth and not merely in appearance, and truly died our common death. Moreover he truly rose from the dead, and after the resurrection companied with his disciples and was then taken up into heaven.

        Then again, the apostles delivered this doctrine, that the Holy Spirit is united in honour and dignity with the Father and the Son. In regard to him it is not yet clearly known whether he is to be thought of as begotten or unbegotten, or as being himself also a Son of God or not; but these are matters which we must investigate to the best of our power from holy scripture, inquiring with wisdom and diligence. It is, however, certainly taught with the utmost clearness in the Church, that this Spirit inspired each one of the saints, both the prophets and the apostles, and that there was not one Spirit in the men of old and another in those who were inspired at the coming of Christ.[2]

        Summary:

53

---

[2]J. Stevenson, *A New Eusebius* (Southhampton, England: Camelot Press, Ltd., 1957), 212–213.

From Preaching to Doctrine

b. The superior remoteness of the Father is really inconceivable, in that thought and intelligence are wholly impotent to go beyond the generation of the Lord; and St. John has admirably confined the conception within circumscribed boundaries by two words, "In the *beginning was* the Word." For thought cannot travel outside "*was*," nor imagination beyond "*beginning*." Let your thought travel ever so far backward, you cannot get beyond the "*was*," and however you may strain and strive to see what is beyond the Son, you will find it impossible to get further than the "*beginning*." True religion, therefore, thus teaches us to think of the Son together with the Father.[3]

Summary:

c. In general, what did the Greek Fathers preach?

[3]Colman J. Barry, OSB, ed., *Readings in Church History* (Westminster, MD: The Christian Classics, Inc., 1985).

The Greek Fathers

Directions: Read the following information about three of the Greek Fathers of the Church.

Origen—Greatest Teacher of Greek Theology

In 185 A.D., Origen was born in Alexandria, Egypt, to a Christian family. At the age of seventeen, he was placed in charge of the catechetical school training adult converts in Christian belief. He studied the Scriptures, Greek philosophy, and many other objects. Soon, the Alexandrian school became famous as an academy of university, teaching many subjects. Origen was the master teacher.

Applying Greek philosophical principles to Christian belief, Origen was the first Christian teacher to develop the Church's doctrines on asceticism (self-denial), the nature of the Trinity, and Christ as the Logos (the Word) of God. His writings number in the thousands. He employed seven stenographers, seven copyists, and many calligraphists. The Hexapla, a six-columned Bible with an equal number of translations, was his most famous work.

Origen ran into difficulty. Some of his writings offended the Bishop of Alexandria. After he was refused ordination to the priesthood because he had castrated himself (supposedly, to prepare for a celibate life), Origen was discharged from Alexandria. After settling in Palestine, he reestablished his school, was ordained a priest, and later, at the age of sixty-seven, was martyred after horrendous torturings.

The later Greek Fathers and Church councils in the fourth and fifth centuries used many of Origen's writings and teachings to develop the doctrines of Christian faith. Yet, in spite of his achievements and even martyrdom, Origen is not recognized as a saint in the Church. This is due to his conflict with the Alexandrian Bishop and his self-mutilation. However, we cannot deny the influence of Origen on the Greek phase of Christianity and his role as one of the earliest Fathers of the Church.

> *If you ask anyone in Constantinople for change, he will start discussing with you whether the Son is begotten or unbegotten. If you ask about the quality of bread, you will get the answer: 'The Father is greater, the Son is less.' If you suggest taking a bath you will be told: 'There was nothing before the Son was created.'*
>
> *—Gregory of Nyssa*

55

From Preaching to Doctrine

St. Athanasius—Champion of Orthodoxy

St. Athanasius (297–373) was Bishop of Alexandria, Egypt. A staunch defender of the Church against the heresy of Arianism, he was exiled five times from his diocese. Athanasius is credited with helping to define the doctrine of the Trinity at the Council of Nicea. His writings also contain the earliest witness to the twenty-seven books of the Christian Scriptures.

St. Basil the Great—Cappadocian Father

St. Basil the Great (329–379) was Bishop of Caesarea in Cappadocia. He is best known for his development of a theology of the Holy Spirit and for his contributions to the development of monasticism in the East. The third section of the Nicene Creed, dealing with the Holy Spirit, is the result of his work.

Different Approaches
to the Same Theology

Directions: Read the following comparison of Greek and Latin Fathers.

In the later part of the third century, Roman Emperor Diocletian divided the Roman Empire into two, each with its own capital-center:

West (Rome)—East (Byzantium)

Christian doctrine in the Western Empire developed and was expressed differently than in the East. Like the Greek Fathers, the Latin Fathers of the West were outstanding teachers, bishops, and scholars. However, Western theology exhibited these distinctive characteristics:

1. The Latin language was used to express Christian doctrine.

2. God was viewed as a lawgiver who judged transgressors from orthodox belief.

3. Philosophy, especially Greek Stoicism, was used to explain theological concepts.

4. The Western Church experienced more persecutions, heresies, and apostasy in its local communities.

All these factors affected how Western theology expressed its beliefs. Since this age overlaps with that of the Greek Fathers, conflicts over language and terminology in doctrines abounded at the Church councils. However, with the guidance of the Holy Spirit, the Church compromised and ratified the teachings that constitute the orthodoxy of Western and Eastern Christianity.

Exercise 31

Augustine

You
made
us for
yourself
and our
hearts find
no peace
until they
rest in
you.

—Augustine

58

Directions: Read the information about St. Augustine, then answer the questions.

St. Augustine was born in 354 A.D. to African parents of Romanized Berber origins in Tagaste, Numidia (modern Algeria). His father was a pagan; his mother, Monica, was a Christian. Although he entered the catechumenate during his childhood, he was not baptized as a Christian until 387. Until that time he undertook a long religious and spiritual pilgrimage with many detours along the way. He kept consort with various mistresses and had a fifteen-year affair which produced a son, Adeodatus. Augustine never married the mother of his child because such a marriage would have prevented his political ambitions from full realization. Clearly, he was not the type of person one would expect to become a great saint of the Church.

In 373, after reading Cicero (a Roman philosopher), Augustine was converted to the love of Divine Wisdom. Augustine saw Divine Wisdom personified as God but was repelled by the apparent barbarism found in the bible. As a result, he converted to Manichaeism because of its stress on asceticism and devotion to Christ. After nine years, he came to distrust some of the heretical claims in Manichaeism and continued his search for truth. Eventually he went to Rome and was soon appointed as a rhetorician at Milan.

While in Milan, he came under the influence of St. Ambrose, who showed that some of the biblical passages that had caused Augustine so much difficulty could be interpreted allegorically. Augustine began to realize that Christianity could be challenging and that he did not have to sacrifice his intelligence to believe in Christ. While in Milan, he had a dramatic conversion experience after reading *Romans 13:13–14*:

Let us conduct ourselves properly as in the day, not in orgies and drunkenness, not in promiscuity and licentiousness, not in rivalry and jealousy. But put on the lord Jesus Christ, and make no provision for the desires of the flesh.

Augustine realized that he had been searching all this time for God. He had searched for God *outside* of himself, using his body and his senses, and had failed to find what he had been looking for. He had searched for God *inside* of himself through the use of his own intellectual powers and had not found what he had been looking for. Finally, he found God through Christ. He found "perfect knowledge" *i.e.*, "a well-founded faith, a joyful hope, and an ardent love." (*The Happy Life*, I, 4. 35)

From Preaching to Doctrine

He was baptized around 387 A.D. After his mother's death in 388, Augustine returned to North Africa and founded a monastic community dedicated to study and contemplation. In 391 he was forced into the priesthood at Hippo (on the northern coast of Africa), where he was consecrated bishop in 396. During his ordained ministry he was a tireless defender of Catholic orthodoxy against the Donatist, Pelagian, and Manichaean heresies.

Augustine was a prolific writer: 113 books, 218 letters, and some 800 sermons. He described his journey of faith in his biographical work, *Confessions*. His other famous work, *City of God*, is a theological reflection on the history of the world and an analysis of salvation through Jesus Christ. Augustine helped to formulate doctrines on the Trinity, original sin, grace, and infant baptism. He is remembered as the greatest of the Church Fathers.

What can his life teach us? There is a famous proverb that states: God writes straight with crooked lines. Augustine's journey in faith was not a smooth one. He searched long and hard for meaning in life. But he never gave up the search. Augustine teaches us never to give up, to look for God's work in our lives continually. No matter what we have done, or thought, or said, we can always reform our lives and try again. Augustine teaches us perseverance.

For Reflection:

1. What does it mean to "put on the Lord Jesus Christ"?

2. For Augustine, perfect knowledge consisted of a well-founded faith, a joyful hope, and an ardent love. Is your faith well-founded? What steps are necessary to insure that faith is well-founded?

3. Are you a joyous and hope-filled person? What situations in the world today are in special need of joy and hope? How can you bring these gifts to the world?

4. What or whom do you love beyond all else? How do you show this love? Where does God fit into the picture?

Jerome

Directions: Read the following information about St. Jerome.

St. Jerome (345–420) was born in Northern Italy to Christian parents. After studying the classical disciplines, he was baptized in Rome. He then journeyed through Gaul (modern France) where he joined an ascetic community and spent a number of years in prayer, solitude, and fasting.

Legend states that Jerome had a vision in 374 A.D. in which he felt criticized for his preoccupation with secular learning. In this vision, he was accused of being a follower of Cicero (a Roman philosopher) and not of Christ. He withdrew into the Syrian desert, mastered Hebrew, and began translating biblical manuscripts.

After his ordination to the priesthood, he was appointed a secretary to Pope Damasus in 382. The pope commissioned Jerome to write an improved translation of the bible. In 386, Jerome retired to a life of seclusion, dedicated to translating the original Hebrew and Greek texts of the Scriptures into Latin. It took him twenty-three years to complete the translation and the result, the *Vulgate* Bible, became the official bible of the Roman Catholic Church. Its use was reaffirmed by the Council of Trent in the 1500s, and it was still in use well into the twentieth century. By far, Jerome was the leading biblical scholar of his time!

Although a biblical scholar and not a theologian, Jerome wrote commentaries on most parts of the bible. His commentaries sought a middle ground between the highly symbolic and the strictly literal methods of biblical interpretation. Like others, Jerome advocated a threefold interpretation of scripture with historical, symbolic, and spiritual meanings.

Jerome's greatest contribution to the Church was in making the scriptures accessible to the people. In his day and age, only those who received a classical education (*i.e.*, those who studied Greek) could read the bible. His translation of the text into Latin (the common language of the empire) enabled all people—from the lowliest slave to the most educated of teachers—to learn about the faith through reading or listening.

It is interesting to note that the New Testament as we have it now was not finalized until about 400 A.D. The chart below traces the history of how the Church came to recognize which books were to be included in the bible.

The early church recognizes the New Testament

A.D. 100

All dates approximate

Different parts of our New Testament were written by this time, but not yet collected and defined as 'Scripture.' Early Christian writers (for example Polycarp and Ignatius) quote from the Gospels and Paul's letters, as well as from other Christian writings and oral sources.

Paul's letters were collected late in the first century. Matthew, Mark and Luke were brought together by A.D. 150.

A.D. 200

New Testament used in the church at Rome
(the 'Muratorian Canon')

Four Gospels
Acts
Paul's letters:
    Romans
    1 & 2 Corinthians
    Galatians
    Ephesians
    Philippians
    Colossians
    1 & 2 Thessalonians
    1 & 2 Timothy
    Titus
    Philemon

James

1 & 2 John
Jude
Revelation of John
Revelation of Peter
Wisdom of Solomon

To be used in private, but not public, worship

The Shepherd of Hermas

A.D. 250

New Testament used by Origen

Four Gospels
Acts
Paul's letters:
    Romans
    1 & 2 Corinthians
    Galatians
    Ephesians
    Philippians
    Colossians
    1 & 2 Thessalonians
    1 & 2 Timothy
    Titus
    Philemon

1 Peter
1 John

Revelation of John

Disputed
Hebrews
James
2 Peter
2 & 3 John
Jude
The Shepherd of Hermas
Letter of Barnabas
Teaching of Twelve
   Apostles
Gospel of the Hebrews

From Preaching to Doctrine

A.D. 300

A.D. 400

New Testament
used by Eusebius

Four Gospels
Acts
Paul's letters:
    Romans
    1 & 2 Corinthians
    Galatians
    Ephesians
    Philippians
    Colossians
    1 & 2 Thessalonians
    1 & 2 Timothy
    Titus
    Philemon

1 Peter
1 John

Revelation of John
(authorship in doubt)

New Testament fixed for
the West by the Council
of Carthage

Four Gospels
Acts
Paul's letters:
    Romans
    1 & 2 Corinthians
    Galatians
    Ephesians
    Philippians
    Colossians
    1 & 2 Thessalonians
    1 & 2 Timothy
    Titus
    Philemon
Hebrews
James
1 & 2 Peter
1, 2 & 3 John
Jude
Revelation

Disputed but well known
James
2 Peter
2 & 3 John
Jude

To be excluded
The shepherd of Hermas
Letter of Barnabas
Gospel of the Hebrews
Revelation of Peter
Acts of Peter
Didache

From Preaching to Doctrine

A Fatherly Review

Part A

Directions: Read the descriptions below and determine which Church father is described in each.

1. _____ As a bishop in Alexandria, Egypt, I was recognized as the outstanding theological authority in the whole Church. I fought against a haughty priest called Arius.

2. _____ I used the phrase *Catholic* to identify Christians all over the Roman Empire. Seven of my letters were passed around to Christian communities. Lions in the Roman amphitheater ate me.

3. _____ In my letter to the Church in Corinth, I indicated the primacy of Rome and the importance of listening to the bishop of Rome.

4. _____ A fiery preacher against heretics, I lived in Bethlehem and wrote the Latin *Vulgate* Bible.

5. _____ At the age of eighteen, I was head of my own school. Some consider me the first great Eastern theologian. I always believed that Jesus was the Savior and tried to explain that, using the philosophy of the Greeks. The Church, however, does not recognize me as a Father of the Church.

6. _____ Bishop of Hippo; and former Manichean; I developed doctrine; I am sometimes considered the greatest Church Father.

7. _____ Some call me the "Father of Eastern Monasticism." I was a master at Byzantine writing, one of the Cappadocian Fathers, yet a humble monk and bishop of Caesarea. My brother Gregory became a bishop.

Part B

Directions: For each person described above, determine whether he is an Apostolic, Greek, or Latin Father.

1. _____   5. _____

2. _____   6. _____

3. _____   7. _____

4. _____

63

A Sign and Instrument of the Kingdom

Part A

Directions: Jesus' mission was to proclaim and bring about the kingdom of God. He did this through his attitudes, his teachings, and his actions. Read and summarize the passages below. Then determine the central idea.

1. **Jesus' Attitudes**

   a. *Mark 6:34*   Summary:

   b. *Luke 15:11–32*   Summary:

   c. *John 8:1–11*   Summary:

   Jesus attitude towards others was . . .

2. **Jesus' Teachings**

   a. *Matthew 5:1–12*   Summary:

   b. *Matthew 5:21–48*   Summary:

   c. *Matthew 6:1–18*   Summary:

   Jesus taught us that . . .

3. **Jesus' Actions**

   a. *Mark 8:1–10*   Summary:

   b. *Luke 8:40–56*   Summary:

   c. *Matthew 26:26–30*   Summary:

   Jesus showed us the power of the kingdom of God by . . .

Part B

Directions: The Church is called to continue Jesus' mission on earth. We are called to the same attitude, understanding of the kingdom of God, and actions. List specific examples of how your parish and the larger Church community continue the mission of Jesus.

1. **Attitudes:** How do your parish and the larger Church show love and compassion toward others?

   Parish   Universal Church

   a.   a.

   b.   b.

   c.   c.

2. **Teachings:** How do your parish and the larger Church inform us about the requirements of the kingdom of God?

   Parish   Universal Church

   a.   a.

   b.   b.

   c.   c.

3. **Actions:** How do your parish and the larger Church act to bring about the kingdom of God?

   Parish   Universal Church

   a.   a.

   b.   b.

   c.   c.

65

One, Holy, Catholic, Apostolic

Directions: Read the clues to determine the correct word to fill-in the blanks.

1. _ _ O _ _ _ _ _
2. _ _ N _ _ _ _ _ _
3. _ _ _ E _ _
4. _ _ _ _ _ H _ _ _ _ _ _ _ _
5. _ _ _ _ O _
6. _ _ _ _ L
7. _ _ _ _ _ _ Y
8. _ _ _ _ _ _ _ _ C _ _ _ _ _ _ _ _ _ _ _
9. _ A _ _ _ _ _ _
10. _ _ _ _ _ _ _ _ T _ _ _ _ _
11. _ _ _ _ _ H
12. _ _ O _ _ _ _
13. _ _ _ L _ _ _ _ _ _ _ _
14. _ I _ _
15. _ _ C _ _ _ _ _ _
16. _ _ A _ _ _
17. _ _ P _
18. _ _ _ _ _ O _
19. _ _ _ _ _ _ S _
20. T _ _ _ _
21. _ O _ _ _ _ _ _ _
22. _ _ _ _ L _
23. _ _ _ _ _ I _ _
24. C _ _ _ _ _

25. _ _ _ , _ _ _ _ , _ _ _ _ _ _ _ _ , _ _ _ _ _ _ _ _ _ _

From Preaching to Doctrine

66

Religion
should be
the rule
of life,
not a
casual
incident
of it.

—Disraeli

Clues: A list of possible answers to the puzzle is provided on page 68.

1. In the Hebrew Scriptures, one who speaks the word of God

2. A type of service performed for the Church community

3. From the word presbyter, a leader of the faith community

4. The collective name for the Apostolic, Greek, and Latin Fathers who helped develop doctrine and lead the Church

5. From the word *episkopos*, an overseer of the community

6. An example; a way of looking at things

7. Officially recognized public worship of God through the sacraments and the recitation of the Holy Hours

8. The unbroken line of authority which can be traced from Peter through all legitimate successors

9. To make holy

10. The scripture passages used to indicate the special role given to Peter by Jesus

11. The local church

12. A collection of parishes under the direction of a bishop

13. The shared responsibility for Church leadership among all bishops

14. In the Hebrew Scriptures, a leader of the people, such as David or Solomon

15. An official teaching of the Church

16. From the word *diakonos*, a helper in the Church

17. The Bishop of Rome

18. Christ's _____ has a Church.

19. The central liturgy, the sacrament of unity

20. To explain what the kingdom of God involves

21. A group of people united for a purpose

22. A model of the Church which focuses on proclaiming the Gospel

23. The Apostolic Father who first used the word *catholic* to describe the Church

24. The offices the pope uses in the administration of the Church

25. The four marks of the Church

From Preaching to Doctrine

Word List

apostolic succession	king
bishop	liturgy
Church Fathers	ministry
collegiality	mission
community	model
curia	parish
deacon	Petrine Texts
diocese	pope
doctrine	priest
Eucharist	prophet
herald	sanctify
Ignatius	teach

The Spiritual Pilgrimage

Directions: St. Augustine described the pilgrimage of faith as including eight basic characteristics. Read each of the passages listed below, and then answer the questions.

1. Thirst for God—*John 4*

2. Delight in Searching for God—*Matthew 13:44–46*

3. Joy in the Truth—*1 Corinthians 13:4–7*

4. Willing Submission to God's Sovereignty—*Colossians 1:15–20*

5. Commitment to Contemplation—*Ephesians 3:14–21*

6. Responsiveness to Neighbors' Needs—*Matthew 25:31–46*

7. Active Participation in the Church's Worship and Work—*Psalm 95:1–7 and 2 Timothy 4:1–5*

8. Unity with All in Charity—*Colossians 3:12–17*

> Only God is unfailing, and even with God we've got to get our criteria straight. God is not bound to support us on the terms that we expect or want. We have to write God a blank check.
>
> —John Carmody

69

From Preaching to Doctrine

1. A journey of a thousand miles begins with a single step, as the saying goes. The first step of a spiritual pilgrimage is to "thirst" for God. What does this mean? In what ways can Jesus quench this thirst?

2. The road is very long, and sometimes we get impatient to get where we are going. Often, we do not find God right away. Why not? How can the searching process be a "delight"? Why?

3. Perhaps we do not really want to know the truth! What if the truth is bad news? Sometimes the truth hurts. Is it possible to be joyful even in these situations?

4. It is not easy to give over our mind and will to God. We have to give God *permission* to work in our lives. What are some of the things that prevent us from turning our lives over to God? What steps can we take to overcome this problem?

5. Prayer, especially contemplation, requires discipline and sustained effort. What situations lead us to prayer? How is contemplation different from vocalized or memorized prayers? What can we do to foster a stronger commitment to our prayer life?

6. True prayer leads to action, and the best actions are those spent in the service of others. What are the most pressing needs of the students in your class today? What are the most pressing needs in your parish? city? country? world? What *concrete* things can you do to respond?

7. For service *to* the community we are called to find strength *within* the community. This is what Church is all about. How do you *actively* participate in worship? What work is your parish doing to bring people closer to God? Are you helping? Why or why not?

8. Christ calls us to love all people, not just our friends. In what ways can we show love to those who are not our friends? How can we show love to our enemies?

The Solitary Life

Directions: Read the following stories about early monasticism.

"... sell all that you have and distribute it to the poor, and you will have a treasure in heaven. Then come, follow me."

—*Luke 18:22p*

1. *St. Antony*, an Anchorite (c. 256–356) and native of Coma in Middle Egypt, was not the first solitary, but he is the most famous and so has become known as the Father of Monasticism.

    Antony heard a sermon about Jesus' call to the rich young man, "If you wish to be perfect, go, sell what you have and give to [the] poor, and you will have treasure in heaven. Then come, follow me" (*Matthew 19:21*). Upon hearing this, Antony sold part of his property. His parents had died, and though he yearned to give his life totally to God, he worried about his sister, for whom he felt responsible. Soon, he heard the Gospel message, "Look at the birds in the sky; they do not sow or reap, they gather nothing into barns, yet your heavenly Father feeds them. Are not you more important than they? ... So do not worry ... Your heavenly Father knows that you need them all. But seek first the kingdom [of God] and his righteousness, and all these things will be given to you besides" (*Matthew 6:26, 31–33*). This led him to sell the remainder of his possessions, give much of the proceeds to the poor and save enough for his sister's future.

    After spending some time studying scripture, while praying and fasting under a holy man, Antony went into the desert, settled in a stone cave where he had access to a spring of water, and lived alone for twenty years, existing on meager produce from a tiny garden he planted. His initial years of solitude were filled with temptations.

    Finally, he emerged from his solitude in response to pleas of those who, impressed by his lifestyle, established hermitages of their own close by. He agreed to guide their growth in spirituality and their search for God.

    People who believed themselves possessed by the devil, as well as those with other physical and mental sufferings, came to him that he might bring the special favor of God into their lives.

    Legend relates how Antony learned from God about Paul, the first Egyptian Anchorite. Antony went on pilgrimage to Paul's cave, and they shared reflections on God's mystery and goodness.

If the world knew our happiness, it would, out of sheer envy, invade our retreats, and the times of the Fathers of the Desert would return when the solitudes were more populous than the cities.

—Sr. Madeleine Sophie Barat

From Preaching to Doctrine

A raven, which had daily brought half a loaf to feed Paul, that day brought a whole loaf, and they thanked God for taking such tender care of His servants.

Before Antony died in very old age, he asked his two most trusted disciples to be sure he was buried in an unidentified spot in the desert, so that those who honored him for his holiness in life might not idolize his lifeless body.

Antony's life was later to play an important role in inspiring Augustine to choose the monastic way of life. Augustine saw true value in the renunciation of one's own will; he thought people should control their instincts rather than *be* controlled by them.

2. **Pachomius** (292–346), a cenobite, was one of Antony's early disciples. Antony at first lived the life of an anchorite; later he became a hermit. By the time of his death, he began to see seeds of a community in the group of disciples who placed themselves under his guidance.

Pachomius, a former soldier who had been impressed by the care the Christians gave local prisoners, began to promote communal living among those who had chosen to be hermits. He decreed that "the monk who does not work will not eat" and introduced a well-organized schedule that included work, prayer, and two meals a day. He tested the sincerity of new applicants by leaving them outside the gate for two days, pleading for admission, while being jostled and pushed around by "the brethren." If they persevered, they were brought in, instructed for a short time by one of the monks, and, finally, given the garb that carried with it the privileges and responsibilities of being part of the community.

Pachomius felt that the discipline of living together was linked to Jesus' commandment that we should fulfill the law by loving one another. This idea spread, and soon a women's cloister (fence or enclosure) was founded by Pachomius's sister. Men's and women's communities generally shunned one another as temptations against their choice (not yet vow) of chastity.

Pachomius's guidelines for community living were written down and became the first formal *rule* for religious life. His community expanded very quickly. Workers of the same occupation (farmers, carpenters, gatekeepers) began to live together in houses with their own superiors. Pachomius was the overall superior. The size of the groups made a personal family lifestyle impossible.

3. **St. Basil of Caesarea** (329–379) was born into an outstanding Christian household. He gave up his popularity as a famous speaker to live a monastic life. His brother had already chosen a way of solitude; after the death of Basil's father, his mother and sister turned their family home into a monastery for women.

Basil visited anchorites and hermits in Egypt and was impressed with their discipline. He was most strongly attracted to Pachomius's communal lifestyle. Referring to Jesus' example of disciples washing one another's feet, he asked, "If one lives alone, whose feet will he wash?" Basil preferred a smaller grouping than Pachomius, as he wished to provide a family atmosphere where he could have a fatherly relationship with each of his monks.

Basil favored a balance of work, prayer, and the study of scripture for his community. He extended the wisdom gained through his monastic experience to the laity by offering classical education to youth. From this period on, Catholic education became increasingly the responsibility of men and women in religious life.

Basil wrote a rule which showed the influence of Pachomius. He advocated greater cooperation with bishops and advised that bishops be chosen from among the monks. After a while, the monks neglected Basil's tradition of educating of youth and caring for the sick. Prayer was emphasized and, in the process, the cenobitical ideal (to love and serve one another) weakened.

4. **St. Benedict** (480–543) was born in Nursia in Italy. His family sent him to Rome to study law and rhetoric, but he gave up the prestige of such a future because of temptations which tended to threaten his faith. He lived in a cave for three years, supplied with food by a holy man whom he had requested to be his spiritual director. At times, he experienced strong desires to return to his former comfortable life, but he mortified his body to strengthen his willpower and obtain from God the grace of perseverance.

Eventually, Benedict moved to a mountain called Monte Cassino, where he lived the last fourteen years of his life. As a result of his preaching, the local people gave up pagan practices and committed themselves anew to Christ. Many went to live with Benedict. All social classes were represented. Benedict, who was familiar with the lifestyle of Antony and Basil, preferred the cenobitical or community life. He rejected the large institutional community associated with Pachomius and kept his communities to a size which he could manage as a family. He wrote a rule that was more sensitive to the western way of life, incorporating more moderate guidelines and demanding less stringent mortifications than the eastern rules. It lent itself to the European temperament and emphasized prayer and work.

From Preaching to Doctrine

Benedict's sister, Scholastica, founded a monastery for women close to Monte Cassino. On the rare occasions when they got together, it is said, they spent hours in sharing their meditations on the wonder of God.

5. *St. Columban of Iona* (c. 543–615) was born of royal blood in Ireland. His family had him educated by priests. After a pilgrimage, Columban founded a number of monasteries for which he created a rule of discipline, apostolic works, study, and prayer. Columban's followers were among the first to practice confession as we know it. They were also among the earliest to solemnize their commitments by taking vows of poverty, celibacy, and obedience.

Columban took with him twelve disciples and went into voluntary exile. Columban and his monks preserved Christianity in Scotland and England.

From Iona, the small island which became their home in exile, Columban and his friends went by boat on missionary expeditions. They converted the invading warlike Picts and worked with nominally Christian Celts to restore the purity of their faith. Columban's name graces the memory of the Irish Church in an age when Ireland was a cultural, intellectual, and religious center of Europe. Scholars from all over Europe, especially England, derived their education from the monks, masters in literary and aesthetic arts.

Columban himself worked tirelessly, both physically, and intellectually. It is said that he made 300 copies of the Gospels. He slept on planks or on the floor with only a rock for a pillow. Because of the monks' desire to educate barbarians and to spread the Gospel, and because of their longing for solitude, Columban and his monks continued to find monasteries in distant and deserted places.

Columban is significant in the intellectual expansion of Europe. He was one of the first in Europe to combine monastic discipline with missionary endeavors. Several centuries later, the Benedictine Rule, including the vow of stability, put an end to the Celtic wandering spirit. In the twelfth and thirteenth centuries, the missionary spirit was resurrected by Saints Francis and Dominic.

The Disaster

Directions: Imagine that a series of earthquakes has just hit the United States. We have suffered extensive damage to land and to population. Major cities have been destroyed. There are no government programs to assist in rebuilding.

You are a Christian survivor who believes God can bring good out of evil or chaos. You also believe that God uses human beings as instruments. A few others who also survived the earthquakes share your beliefs. They are willing to work together to put these beliefs into practice.

You have found records of a Christian monastic sect that once helped civilize the world. Write a rule of life for yourself and the others based on the life of the monk you have just studied. Make sure your rule will help you both to live your Christian beliefs and to survive in a difficult environment.

Some things to think about: What do you believe about yourselves? About God? About your place in the rest of the world? Who is in charge? How is the day-to-day business of your community to be carried out? What will you eat? When? How will you support yourselves? What will you wear? Where will you find these clothes? What will you do about those who do not follow the rules? What will you do about those who want to join?

It is more difficult, and calls for higher energies of soul, to live a martyr than to die one.

—Horace Mann

75

The Rise of Islam

Directions: Read the following summary of the development of Islam.

In the seventh century, the Roman Empire was devastated by barbarian invasions, and the Eastern Empire and Church established itself as a unique entity. Far to the southeast in the Arabian peninsula, a new religious movement was awakening. The rise of the Islamic (Muslim) faith was about to pose a new challenge to Christian beliefs in both the East and the West. This new Arabian religion founded by Muhammad spread quickly. Like Christians and Jews, Muslims believed in God and his prophets; however, there were many differences. Islam developed into a cultural expression unifying the Arabian tribes and challenging the world with its doctrines. From the eighth to the twelfth centuries, Islam became the religious and cultural giant of the Middle East, North Africa, and the Iberian peninsula. It was involved in worldwide conflicts with Christians from the Carolingian period through the Crusades.

Around 580, Mahommet (better known to us as Muhammad) was born of poor parents in Mecca, a little town in Arabia. He earned his living as a caravaneer in the employ of a widow whom he married when he was twenty-five and she forty. On his travels, he talked with Christians and Jews and was drawn to the concept of one God. Muhammad's religious reflections convinced him that he was a prophet chosen to preach about this one God, Allah, whom he associated with Abraham, to whose first son, Ishmael, Muhammad's tribe, traced their origin. Islam asks belief in the prophet Muhammad and in rituals prescribed in the Koran (Islamic scriptures) compiled from Muhammad's teachings. The unlettered could easily grasp the message.

His emphasis on responsibility for the poor led Muhammad's townspeople to reject him, and he fled to Medina in 622 A.D. This event, remembered as the Hegira, is the officially recognized date for the founding of Islam. Justice to the poor and orphans was stressed, but vengeance was also allowed. Though Muhammad's original plan did not include missionary wars, his teaching that the supreme offering is the sacrifice of one's life for Allah was an incentive to this kind of expansion. One reason for the great impact of the Muslim army on the Christianized world was the first feat of Muhammad: he united hordes of wandering Arabs along the Arabian Peninsula, and their strength surprised even themselves. At first, the Islamic faith spread through arduous travels and preaching, but soon these tactics changed. Military expeditions were initiated; these proved immensely more effective.

Within 100 years of Muhammad's birth, Muslims had conquered the entire Persian Empire, Egypt, Palestine, Syria, Roman Africa, Spain, Southern France, and the Mediterranean islands. In 717, Leo III, the Emperor of Constantinople, stalled their advance to that city, and Charles Martel became a hero in the West by his devastating defeat of the Muslims at Portiers, France, in 732, the hundredth anniversary of Muhammad's death.

By this time Islam was experiencing internal problems. Members lost the original purity of faith; small pockets of rebellion were organized by Christians and began to take firm root. Spain was the last of Islam's big conquests. Christian civilization reestablished its power; the reconquest of the Spanish Peninsula testified to this fact. The situation stabilized until the eleventh century, when radical Muslims conquered and desecrated Christian shrines in the Holy Land, leading to the crusades.

77

The Pillars of Islam

Directions: The central beliefs of Islam, the youngest of the major world religions, are summarized in the Five Pillars of Islam, which Muslims hold sacred. Read the following description of the fundamental beliefs.

Pillar 1: Belief— "There is no God, except Allah, and Muhammad is the prophet of Allah."

Allah— is the Islamic name for the one, only, true God.

— God's timeless knowledge controls all events in life.

— Angels help minister Allah's word.

Prophets— In the Islamic view of religion, Muhammad is the last of a long line of Allah's prophets.

— The first prophet was Abraham, the "Father of all Faiths," to whom trace their heritage through Ishmael, the son of Hagar, the handmaid of Sarah.

— Jesus was a great prophet, born of the Virgin Mary, but not God or God's Son.

Pillar 2: Prayer— Devout Muslims must pray towards Mecca, Saudi Arabia, five times daily.

— Muslims are called to prayer by a Muezzin or crier from a minaret (a tall tower) which is part of the architecture of a mosque.

— Friday is considered a special day of prayer and rest for all Muslims. At noon, the men gather at the mosque for prayers.

Pillar 3: Fasting— One month every year, Ramadan, is set aside for fasting.

— Muslims are required to abstain from all food, drink, smoking, and sex from sun-up to sun-down during Ramadan.

— The pangs of hunger and thirst help devout Muslims identify more closely with the poor.

Pillar 4: Almsgiving— Also called Zakat, poordue, or purity, is the offering of a percent of one's income for the poor.

— Giving to the poor is considered a religious duty to Allah, a form of worship.

Pilliar 5: Pilgrimage— Every year a three-day period is established for the Haj—a religious pilgrimage to Mecca and Medina, Saudi Arabia.

— This pilgrimage is required once in a Muslim's lifetime.

— Special clothing, rituals, and prayers are followed throughout the three-day period.

From Preaching to Doctrine

Islam and Christianity—A Comparison

Directions: Islam is the youngest of the major world religions. *Islam* means "peace through faith and surrender to Allah." *Muslim* means "one who submits to (the will of) Allah."

Today, with nearly 900 million followers, Islam is the largest single world religion.

Using the information on the Five Pillars of Islam (**Exercise 40**) compare Islamic practice with Christian practices.

	Islam	Christianity
Pillar 1: Belief		
Pillar 2: Prayer		
Pillar 3: Fasting		
4: Almsgiving		
5: Pilgrimage		

Always remember, my king, that you are the deputy of God, your King. You are set to guard and rule all his members, and you must render an account for them on the day of judgment. The bishop is on a secondary plane.

—Epistolae
Karolini Aevi

79

From Preaching to Doctrine

80

Part 3

From Monarchy to Reform

But you are "a chosen race, a royal priesthood, a holy nation, a people of his own, so that you may announce the praises" of him who called you out of darkness into his wonderful light.

—*1 Peter 2:9*

Historians sometimes call the next period of history the Dark Ages. Indeed, in some respects the times were dark, and for the Church there was a great deal of confusion. Yet night is the prelude to dawn, and new life can emerge after a period of darkness. We will, therefore, look at this period as one of preparation, a time of building foundations which would eventually support a whole society—the Christian Middle Ages.

Politically, this was a time of chaos. In the West, the Roman Empire was falling apart, something incomprehensible to a world view that saw Rome as an unchangeable hub. Into the vacuum left by imperial Rome stepped some remarkable popes who found ways to keep the Church—and society itself—afloat during the floods of invaders who moved into Western Europe. Through these popes, forward-looking leadership, the Church, which had been city-centered, learned to operate in the countryside. It brought new groups into the Church and learned to adapt customs from Germanic cultures to the faith.

Eventually, Roman popes and Western rulers produced some stability by supporting one another, since each had difficulty functioning alone. Together this Church/State partnership faced additional difficulties during a new wave of invaders from the north. The Vikings' swift movement down the waterways of both Eastern and Western Europe caused much uproar and brought new opportunities for Christianity to convert more people.

In the East, the Roman Empire survived longer under the name of the Byzantine Empire. Outwardly at least it was much grander and more stable than the government in the West. It followed the pattern set by Constantine—a strong emperor who controlled both Church and State to maintain unity. But it had its own set of problems, for heresy continued to threaten it. Its form of Christianity, therefore, developed along other paths than Christianity in the West, causing mutual misunderstanding.

· Christianity in both its Eastern and Western forms, found different ways to survive difficulties. This would prove to be their undoing as well. These two expressions of Christianity became too different to stay united.

The Medieval Concept of Christendom

Directions: Read the following description of the shifting relationship between Church and State during the Middle Ages.

The Holy Roman Emperor

Vast differences developed between Christianity in the East and Christianity in the West. In the East, the emperor in Constantinople controlled the church which paced heresies and the spread of Islam. In the West, meanwhile, different pressures were building. Islam was stopped by Charles Martel in 732 and the pope in Rome had the prestige of being acknowledged as the head of the Church. He even took over by default some functions of the emperor, such as paying soldiers and running the city of Rome. However, as the barbarians chipped away at the remaining influence of the empire in the West, the pope was left in a difficult position.

The pope was physically threatened by the Lombards, a Germanic tribe which invaded Italy. At the same time, he cut off any chance of support from the East by challenging the Greek emperor about the issue of icons. The only refuge from his troubles seemed to be in the Frankish kingdom to the northwest (modern France). This tribe had converted to Christianity in the fifth century when their king, Clovis, was baptized. Later it was the Franks that were responsible for stopping Islam's advance into the West. So it was to the Franks that the pope turned for a relationship which could be of mutual benefit.

This relationship formed the philosophical foundation of the Middle Ages. This foundation was called *Christendom*, a worldview that believed that Church and State should operate together; they were to support and enhance each other. The result was one Church and one State; to belong to one meant automatically to belong to the other.

Pope Zacharias and his successor Pope Stephen planted the seeds of Christendom when they reached out to the Frankish king. Pepin the Short, for assistance. Pepin, the son of Charles Martel, became the sole leader of the Franks in 747. However, his hold on power was not complete, as there were people who questioned his claim to the throne. When the popes asked for help, Pepin saw a chance for mutual support.

Popes Zacharias and Stephen supported Pepin's claim to kingship. They also had him anointed and crowned. This was to establish him as legitimate ruler who could not be challenged. In return, Pepin sent an army to defeat the Lombards; he then gave the pope the conquered territory. This "Donation of Pepin" became the basis for the Papal States, which were governed by popes until 1870. Vatican City today is the only remnant left of this once great territory.

Pepin's son, Charlemagne (768–814), expanded Pepin's claims. Charlemagne was six feet tall; he literally towered over his contemporaries. His ego and ambitions matched his physical size. On the positive side, he was a good soldier and an excellent administrator. These abilities helped him as he moved east and south, conquering new areas for his kingdom. He was moderate in eating and drinking. He was also very religious. On the dark side, however, he was cruel and autocratic. People he conquered were forced to be baptized or die. While emphasizing Christian principles, he was unfaithful in his own marriage.

The mutual support plan begun by Pepin continued. Pope Leo III offered his support to Charlemagne's claim to kingship. This was eventually cemented in a ceremony in Rome in which Leo crowned Charlemagne as the Roman emperor on Christmas Day, 800 A.D. By this action, Charlemagne became the successor of the earlier Roman emperors, not just king. In return, Charlemagne supported reform in the Church and gave the Church financial aid through a system of taxes called tithes.

The balance soon tipped in Charlemagne's favor. Mutual support turned to domination of religious affairs by Charlemagne. As he conquered, Charlemagne created new dioceses and assigned bishops; he also established monasteries and built churches. He began giving bishops political and civil powers besides their religious duties. He even called synods (meetings of bishops) and helped in making decisions. He legislated how Mass was to be celebrated and demanded that clergy in his kingdom be educated and taught to preach well. Education was important to him, and brought many scholars to live at his court. The most famous of these teachers were Bede and Alcuin, both from England. In his view of this mutual support system, he was to be the ringmaster while the pope was to pray for the success of the show!

After Charlemagne's death, the kingdom quickly fell apart. It was divided by his children and grandchildren into ever-smaller pieces. However. the legacy of a Roman emperor ruling over a united Christendom—one Church, one State—was to remain alive for a very long time. It would have far-reaching effects on the Pilgrim Church.

Cluniac Reforms

Within Christendom, individual feudal kingdoms remained and continued to fight with each other. These civil wars had devastating effects on the innocent commoners. Unexpectedly, a mounted knight and army would ride up to confiscate cattle and property and press young men into armed service. Religious pilgrimages were interrupted by feudal wars. The popes eventually took leadership, suggesting a cessation to warfare under a program called *Peace of God*. Under this, feudal lords swore agreement to a treaty which prohibited attacks on serfs, clergy, women, and pilgrims. Neither protected persons nor their property could be harmed under the agreement. Furthermore, cathedrals, churches, and monasteries were protected from being despoiled by feudal armies. Feudal lords who broke the "Peace of God" were excommunicated. This meant they and their family were denied the sacraments, including Christian burial.

Soon the treaty was expanded into the *Truce of God.* This expanded version condemned warfare from sundown on Wednesday until sun-up on Monday. Fighting during Advent and Lent and on holy days was strictly forbidden. Lords swore to uphold these limiting norms under pain of excommunication or interdict. (Interdict meant that no church services or sacraments would be permitted in the feudal fiefdom.) Local bishops supervised and enforced the dictates of these treaties. Unfortunately, the treaties worked better in theory than in practice.

Growth of Papal Power

As Hildebrande, the Cluniac monk who had advised Pope Leo IX, Gregory VII (1073–1085) received the pallium (a vestment worn by popes as symbol of their papal office) and found a Church once again in need of reform. During two Roman synods early in his reign, decrees were enacted to again stamp out simony, married clergy, and lay investiture. In the eleventh century, the authority of the pope was not universally recognized. Bishops were often caught in a catch-22 position, allegiance to the pope or fealty and loyalty to the local prince who had invested them with miter and crozier. In 1075, Pope Gregory issued a ruling on the problem of lay investiture. In Dictates of the Pope (*Dictatus Papae*), he stated:

1. Only popes can depose bishops.

2. Only a pope may use imperial insignia.*

3. No one has the authority to judge the pope's rulings.

4. A pope may dispense lords/vassals from loyalty to a sinful emperor/king.

With this ruling a new battle line was drawn. Who was more powerful—pope or prince? Bishops who refused to comply with Gregory's dictates were stripped of their ecclesiastical offices. A war was about to begin.

85

---

*   Imperial insignia—a special vestment, probably a pallium, worn to signify authority passed down from the days of emperial Rome

At the turn of the twelfth century, the battle over lay investiture diminished because of the Concordat of Worms in 1122. Henceforth, bishops and other clergy were to receive spiritual appointments from the Church, but the emperor/king could invest them with temporal signs of office. Pope Innocent III (1198–1216) sensed in the papacy a moral force for society. He used excommunication, interdict, and papal taxation to reform the morality of the monarchies of Fredrick II (Barbarosa) of Germany, Philip Augustus of France, and King John of Runneymeade. The highlight of his reign was the inauguration of the Fourth Lateran Council in 1215, the most important council of the Middle Ages.

The reforming canons of the Lateran Council solidified papal authority. The 70 Canons of the Council included clear statements on such matters as

- Eliminating clerical abuses and simony

- Condemning heresies

- Requiring papal approval of new religious orders, relics, and the canonization of saints

- Establishing seven official sacraments in the Church

- Requiring all Catholics to confess their sins and receive the Holy Eucharist at least once a year at Easter time (Confessors were put under "the seal" never to reveal what they heard in confession.)

- Defining the Eucharistic doctrine of transubstantiation, stating that at the time of consecration the bread and wine are changed into the real body and blood of Jesus Christ.

These conciliar positions reflect the spiritual and moral fiber of the papal presider Innocent III. The greatest Medieval council was led by one of the best Medieval popes, a guiding light for the pilgrim people of God.

Feudalism and Christendom

Part A

Directions: In each blank, fill in the correct name. Then find the names in the wordsearch block below. Words can be found going up, down, diagonally, or backwards.

1. The Franks had been Christian since the fifth century when_____, their king, was baptized.

2. Charles _____ defeated the Muslims in the West.

3. _____ gave the Papal States to the pope.

4. Pope _____ III crowned Charlemagne Roman emperor.

5. The _____ threatened the popes physically.

6. St. _____ wrote *The City of God*.

7. _____thought that he should make all decisions

8. while the _____should pray for his success.

9. _____and

10. _____were two English scholars Charlemagne brought to his court.

K	G	D	L	P	O	P	E	R	A	I	P
B	D	T	S	M	A	C	U	V	T	H	C
L	E	T	R	A	M	S	P	N	C	H	I
O	I	B	U	N	D	F	H	S	A	J	E
M	K	R	L	I	A	E	I	R	V	W	N
B	E	D	E	F	C	V	L	I	G	N	I
A	J	O	A	K	O	E	N	H	D	P	T
R	H	S	T	L	M	U	R	D	W	E	S
D	F	I	C	A	C	E	L	E	O	P	U
S	E	T	G	R	G	U	L	J	M	I	G
A	S	N	V	C	E	H	I	L	O	N	U
A	E	D	O	Q	Y	T	V	N	C	E	A

From Monarchy to Reform

Part B

Directions: Define each of the following terms.

1. Feudalism—

2. Lay investiture—

3. Excommunication—

4. Interdict—

5. Pallium—

Part C

Directions: Answers the questions below in essay form.

1. Explain how *Peace of God* and *Truce of God* curbed medieval warfare.

2. How did the powers of excommunication and interdict help strengthen a declining papacy and weaken the power of the warring feudal lords?

3. What sacramental teachings of the Fourth Lateran Council are actively practiced by Catholics today?

88

Treason in the Ranks

Directions: Read the following summary of the development of the inquisition.

Betrayal is one of the greatest emotional injuries a human being can inflict, and treason is one of the most serious crimes a person can commit. Severe penalties for treason are not considered cruel or unusual punishment as defined by most modern governments.

Twentieth-century students of Church history confront some cruel, barbaric conditions of the past. Catholics may hear comments like, "How can the Catholic Church be true when it gave birth to something as horrible as the Inquisition?" This lesson will examine that question. It will also look at why the Inquisition began and how it operated.

Certainly, the fifteenth-century Spanish Inquisition is a black mark on the record of the Catholic Church. Because Jesus chose human beings to continue His work, human weakness and sin get well mixed into the story of the Church. The wheat and the weeds grew together and they will continue to do so. The excesses of the Spanish Inquisition and its mistreatment of Muslims and Jews in Spain were inexcusable. The earlier papal courts of Inquisition, however, began in the thirteenth century and arose as a response to a serious threat.

The Inquisition began because of two heresies sweeping the Church. In the Christendom of the Middle Ages, there was no separation between Church and State. Questioning the Church automatically meant questioning society itself. The logical conclusion was that a heretic was engaged in treason, the most serious crime against social order. Furthermore, because God was the whole reason behind the establishment of society, to be a heretic meant one betrayed God himself, not just mere humans. What could be more serious to a medieval person?

Manicheism cropped up again in a new form in the thirteenth-century Western Church. It was known as Albigensianism after Albi, a town in southern France which was a stronghold of this heresy. It was also called Catharism from a Greek word meaning "pure." Its teachings attracted people partly because luxurious living by Church leaders scandalized simple town dwellers who saw in Catharism a purer form of Christianity.

The Albigensians taught that there were two gods. The God of the New Testament was spiritual and good; Jehovah, the God of the Old Testament, was the creator of the material world and bad. Denial of anything physical or material was stressed. Marriage and having children were bad. Eating meat, eggs, milk, and cheese were wrong because they were products of reproduction. Sacraments were denied because they used "evil" material symbols, To kill any living thing was wrong because living things were believed to be reincarnated after death; anything killed would be reincarnated as a lesser being.

From Monarchy to Reform

> *We have enough religion to make us hate, but not enough to make us love one another.*
>
> —*Swift*

89

How did this severe heresy survive and become such a problem? In Albigensianism, there were two groups—"believers" and "perfect ones." "Believers," the most numerous group, lived ordinary lives but honored the "perfect ones" and expressed Catharist beliefs. Only "perfect ones" lived severe ascetic lives. A person became a "perfect one" in a ceremony called "consolamentum." Usually, this was put off until a person was close to death. To die a "perfect one" meant an end of the cycle of reincarnation and the beginning of a glorious new life.

The Waldensians, a small group that still survives today, stressed extreme poverty to the point of not owning any possessions and living a strictly communal life. They were founded by Peter Waldo, a rich man from Lyons, France. After reading the Gospel, Waldo sold everything he owned and lived in complete poverty. He got an educated priest to translate the Gospels from Latin into the spoken language of the people (vernacular). He and his followers then memorized large portions of scripture and began preaching and encouraging others to do the same. They believed lay people should also be allowed to administer sacraments. When told by Church authorities to stop these activities, they refused. This refusal to obey made them different from Francis of Assisi and his friars.

When several other attempts failed to stop the spread of these heresies, Pope Gregory IX called for an Inquisition in 1233. In his decree, the pope called for the establishment of courts answerable to the pope alone. These courts were unique in that they moved from town to town under the direction of a chief inquisitor, usually a Dominican friar. Their purpose was two-fold: to convert the heretic from his false belief and certain damnation; if this effort failed, to protect society by punishing the heretic.

After arriving in a town, the court set out to determine names of suspected heretics. It was considered a serious duty to report anyone suspected of heretical activity. The suspects were then brought to court to answer charges. Next, suspects were asked to name anyone they considered an enemy. Secret witnesses could be used against a suspect; if a named person was on the list of witnesses, this person's testimony was eliminated. Later, torture was added as a means of determining guilt. Lastly, those found guilty were given punishments. These ranged from a moderate penance to those showing remorse up to imprisonment for life or even death by burning at the stake for serious offenders.

Certainly, by our standards of justice, these methods and punishments seem unjust. By the standards of the Middle Ages, however, they were moderate and ordinary. Bernard Gui, an inquisitor whose records reveal much about the workings of these courts, was the most criticized judge. Between 1308 and 1323 he convicted 930 people of heresy; of these 42 were executed. As a last resort to eliminate the problem of heresy, the Inquisition was successful.

How the Inquisition Operated

Directions: On the lines below, list in order the procedure followed by the papal Inquisition. Begin with the arrival of the court in a medieval town.

1. _____

    _____

    _____

    _____

    _____

2. _____

    _____

    _____

    _____

    _____

3. _____

    _____

    _____

    _____

    _____

4. _____

    _____

    _____

    _____

    _____

5. _____

    _____

    _____

    _____

    _____

A Day at the Inquisition

Directions: Below are five dialogues expressing possible cases that might have been judged in an inquisition. Read each case and decide what heresy is involved. Put the name of the heresy on the first line. Then decide why the person is accused of that heresy and fill in the second line with your reason. Then answer the questions that follow.

Case 1 _____

      Gui: According to sworn testimony given this court, you refused to bring your child to church for Baptism.

Defendant: That is true, My Lord. Use of water in this way would contaminate my child's innocence.

      Gui: Unless you change your ways and bring your child to your parish priest for the holy sacrament, I declare that you are a(n)_____because _____

_____ .

Case 2 _____

      Gui: At the last holyday festival, you refused to join others in eating the fresh meat prepared for the feast. To refuse this rare treat was rude. Besides, do you understand that this also makes you a suspected heretic?

Defendant: Honorable Lord, I was simply not hungry that day.

      Gui: Nonsense! On the contrary, your beliefs prevented you from eating meat. You are_____because _____

_____ .

Case 3 _____

      Gui: Witnesses have accused you of reciting Holy Scripture in the language of the people right on the public square.

Defendant: Most holy friar, the gospel of Jesus says, "Judge not that you may not be judged."

      Gui: Since you mock me by quoting Jesus' holy words, you indeed are guilty of being_____because _____

_____ .

Case 4 _____

  Gui: You, sir, were seen walking about the street naked. This
has caused your neighbors to gossip and wonder about
your devotion to the true faith.

Defendant: Respectfully, Your Honor, I am just doing what the
Gospel of Jesus has told me I must do—"go sell what
you have and give to [the] poor, . . . " *Matthew 19:21*

  Gui: My dear man, if you are not insane, you must
be _____ because _____

_____ .

Case 5 _____

  Gui: Young woman, you were observed crying when you ac-
cidentally stepped on a cockroach scurrying across the
floor. This behavior is strange for one who claims to be a
Catholic.

Defendant: I have a great respect for life. Is this wrong for a Christian to believe?

  Gui: Your sharp tongue itself betrays you! Now kill this
chicken here before me that it may be given to a poor
starving family.

Defendant: I cannot and will not!

  Gui: Your guilt is sealed! Obviously you _____
because _____

_____ .

1. What punishment might be given each of these people?

2. What factors would decide the severity of the punishment?

East and West—
Growing Misunderstanding

Directions: Read about the growing misunderstandings between Eastern and Western Christianity; then complete the exercise.

Gregory I and other popes in Rome were struggling to keep the Church alive in the West during an era of chaos and invasion. Meanwhile, in the East, the Church was operating in very different environment. These differences led to clashes that seemed relatively minor in the beginning but eventually led to complete separation of the two churches in the schism of the eleventh century.

The emperors that followed Constantine tried to maintain the unity of the Empire. Some were more successful than others. Theodosius (379–395) took Constantine's plan of favoring Christianity further and made it the official religion of the Empire. He went so far as to forbid paganism and persecute heretics, especially Arians.

Perhaps the most successful of the rulers were Justinian (527–565) and his wife, Theodora. His domain was no longer called the Roman Empire, but, instead, the Byzantine Empire (after Byzantium, the site of Constantinople). Theodora was a woman of unusual power and influence. While Justinian was working to undermine heresies in order to maintain unity, his wife secretly financed these heresies by sponsoring a missionary trip of Monophysite monks.

The Justinian Code completed what Constantine began by incorporating Christianity into the laws of the State. Justinian also continued the hold Greek emperors had over the Church by ordering laws regulating its affairs. One of his lasting achievements was the building of the church of Saint Sophia (Holy Wisdom) which still dominates the skyline of Istanbul, the modern name for Constantinople. It is now an Islamic museum. Nothing, though, even the stripping of this church by various invading armies, has destroyed the power and beauty of what Justinian created. Its majesty is a summary of all that was good about Byzantine culture.

Constantinople became a city of great significance. Its strength was expressed in the missionaries it sent north to the Balkans and Russia, east as far as China, and south into North Africa. It also became a center of theological learning and debate. From its emphasis on ritual and symbolism, many traditions have developed and thrived.

In the West, then, the Church was beginning to take over the functions of the state, which was collapsing; in the East the emperor was freely taking over many functions of the Church. This difference caused misunderstanding and conflict between the pope in Rome and the emperor in Constantinople.

Other issues continued to build mistrust between the two sides. The vast geographical distances and different languages (Latin in the West, Greek in the East) were significant. Also, in the East there had always been the Greek tradition of careful use of language in religious matters; riots actually started over the use of certain words and phrases. Heresies continued to cause problems in the East but not in the West. Different customs of worship developed, too. Byzantine culture emphasized elaborate rituals, use of icons, and bread made with yeast.

These and other differences built up over time until the disastrous break in 1054. Despite this separation, some Eastern Churches maintained ties with Rome. These churches are still alive and active today. While numerically small, they contribute much beauty and insight to the faith we all share.

1. On the lines below, list differences between Eastern and Western Christianity.

   a. _____

   _____

   b. _____

   _____

   c. _____

   _____

   d. _____

   _____

   e. _____

   _____

   f. _____

   _____

2. Decide which two differences were most important, and explain why.

95

Rites in the Church

Directions: There are many different expressions of Catholicism. All these expressions are based upon different cultures and ritual practices. Below is a chart of the different expressions of Catholicism. Each separate expression is called a rite. You will notice that the Roman rite is only one way to be Catholic. Study the chart, and then answer the questions.

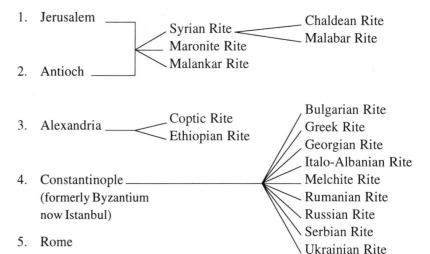

1. Jerusalem
   Syrian Rite — Chaldean Rite
   Maronite Rite — Malabar Rite
   Malankar Rite
2. Antioch

3. Alexandria — Coptic Rite
   Ethiopian Rite

4. Constantinople
   (formerly Byzantium
   now Istanbul)

   Bulgarian Rite
   Greek Rite
   Georgian Rite
   Italo-Albanian Rite
   Melchite Rite
   Rumanian Rite
   Russian Rite
   Serbian Rite
   Ukrainian Rite

5. Rome

1. How many rites are there in the Catholic Church?

2. Look at the place where the rites were originated.
   What do these places have in common?

3. Which place is responsible for the development of the most rites? Why?

The Road Divided

Directions: Read about the Schism of 1054 below. Then complete the exercise.

The great Schism of 1054 ruptured the troubled unity between the church in the West and the church in the East.

Most relationships have ups and downs. In a healthy relationship, hurts and misunderstandings are usually brought into the open and healed in loving ways. At times, though, the damage is irreparable, especially if there have been acts of disloyalty, ignoring of difficulties, or name-calling. Sometimes, it only takes a spark to cause a major blow-up and destroy a relationship.

This happened to the Catholic Church in the eleventh century. A break or separation occurred between the Eastern and Western branches of Christianity. What happened was caused by two very stubborn people, Michael Cerularius and Cardinal Humbert. Over nine-hundred years later the damage has not yet been repaired. Today the Eastern Churches which do not acknowledge the pope as leader of the Church are called Orthodox Churches.

The following monologues provide information about the schism.

Michael Cerularius,
Patriarch of Constantinople

> As the leader of Constantinople, I have been named protector of Christian belief. So many people come along with strange ideas that destroy the true faith. I cannot permit this to happen! I have an obligation!
>
> The people I really detest are those westerners who think they know everything. Just because they come from the pope in Rome, they think they speak with the authority of Jesus himself. What heresy; their pride makes me sick! They do not understand the importance of Constantinople in the empire. This city is the last Christian stronghold left against the Muslims. Furthermore, the Romans' religious beliefs have been barbarized and contaminated by uncivilized pagan tribes. The popes have crowned them as Western emperors making a monarchy out of the Church.
>
> The form of Christianity in the West is a disgrace. They use Latin in their liturgy and bible instead of Greek, the language of the Christian Scriptures. Their bread is flat and tasteless, and, naturally the symbolism Jesus intended is lost; real bread is the only way to show that Jesus gave us food to satisfy our souls.

The Western ways must be forbidden in the East. Maybe I can get the representatives the pope has sent to do something.

Cardinal Humbert, Representative of Pope Leo IX

The patriarch needs to be taught a lesson. Like all Greeks, he thinks he has a corner on what it means to be Catholic. The Greeks are constantly splitting hairs over little things and letting big things get out of control. While they argue about one word in the Creed, they allow the emperor to run things instead of letting the Church have control over the situation. I've traveled a long time to get here to talk to the patriarch. The weather has been miserable and I am exhausted. I was greeted by the closing of churches using Western customs.

I am the pope's representative, and Rome has jurisdiction over Constantinople. Constantinople can never claim to be the home of any of the twelve apostles. The patriarch needs to be put in his place!

Imagine an ending to this confrontation. What might each man do? How might each react? What feelings do you think would be expressed? Include in your presentation some reactions from the people of Constantinople. How do you think the people would feel about this situation? Whom would they support? Why? What do you think they would do?

Crusader Pilgrimages

Directions: Read the following information about the crusades of Christians against Muslims.

a. Call to Military Pilgrimage

Two medieval movements, the pious pilgrimage and feudal warfare, converged into a "holy" union by the calling of the first crusade. Pope Urban II's inspiring call-to-arms against a common enemy to recapture Jerusalem and the Holy Lands was primarily an attempt to curb feudal wars. His impassioned plea at the Council of Clermont in 1095 also inspired the council fathers to declare the "Truce of God" treaties as part of Canon law. The feudal lords were restricted from fighting among themselves but the Crusade gave them an outlet to practice warfare with the Church's blessing. Pope Urban promised the crusaders absolution from excommunication and a plenary indulgence if they would successfully take Jerusalem or die trying.

Thus, the call to crusade ("take up the cross") against the infidel Seljuk Turks (called Saracens by Eastern Christians) was initiated as a Church-sponsored military pilgrimage. The battle cry, "God wills it," incited the fervor and passion of lords, knights, and would-be-soldiers. Europeans sewed the distinctive red crusader cross over their tunics and affixed it to their shields.

b. What Really Started the Crusader Movement?

Late in 1095, an old man, Peter the Hermit, arrived in Europe carrying a letter from the Patriarch of Jerusalem requesting immediate aid. Muslim Turks were besieging Christian holy places. One account reported that a certain caliph commanded the tomb of Jesus inside the Church of the Holy Sepulchre to be destroyed with chisel and hammer. Peter the Hermit, not waiting for papal approval, personally raised a people's army of 15,000 armed pilgrims. This poorly organized "People's Crusade," lacking sound military leadership, was wiped out by the Saracens at Civiltot in Asia Minor (Turkey) in less than three months.

When men are hot with drinking wine

And idly by the fire recline,

They take the cross with eager boast

To make a great crusading host.

But with first glow of morning light

The whole Crusade dissolves in flight.

—Anonymous

99

c. The First Official Crusade

About a year later Pope Urban issued his call-to-arms. It took the crusaders almost two years to fight their way across Asia Minor and Western Syria. With a force of 50,000 trained, well-armed soldier-knights, they were to capture the Saracen strongholds of Edessa, Antioch, Tripoli, and finally Jerusalem in 1099. The crusader leaders set up Christian states centered at captured strongholds and collectively called Outremer (the land "beyond the seas"). This was to be the only really successful crusade. It brought the Holy Lands under European control for a limited time. Over the next 200 years, various parts of the outremer were recaptured by the Muslims.

d. Seven Other Crusades

From 1100–1270 seven more crusading pilgrimages were undertaken to the Latin states of the East. Most of them tried unsuccessfully to recapture crusader kingdoms lost to various Muslim groups. Some crusaders actually settled in the East, raised their families, and managed the land as feudal estates. Not all Muslims were hostile to the Christian settlers, and Europe actually benefited from these associations in commerce, trade, and the exchange of cultures.

To support crusader armies, a series of fortresses and castles were built in a distinctive style across Asia Minor, Syria, and Palestine. Priests and bishops were brought along on the campaigns to provide sacramental support, giving the "armies of the cross" a sense of spiritual mission. Once established in the Holy Lands, churches, shrines, and chapels were built on every location that the clergy believed corresponded to Gospel events. Pious European pilgrims traveled the new trade routes to worship at these holy sites. Many of these crusader structures across Asia Minor (Turkey). Syria, and in Palestine are still standing.

Results of Crusades

From a military standpoint, the Christian crusades were failures. The loss of life, the greed and corruption, and the strain on East/West relationships could not justify the seemingly noble purposes of these Christian wars. In the long run, however, the crusades did contribute a few positive elements to medieval society:

a. The crusades opened up a new world outside of Europe. Provincial feudal lords shifted their bloodlust away from one another.

b. New trade routes were established in the East, providing new commerce, new merchandise, and new business opportunities. Port cities in southern Europe flourished. Economic growth was experienced throughout Europe.

c. Through contact with Muslim culture. Europe advanced intellectually, including the discovery of higher mathematics, advanced sciences, and the writings of ancient Greek philosophers.

d. The founding of knightly orders such as the Hospitalers, Templars and the Teutonic Order and Maltese Cross instituted a new chapter of Christian warfare. It also fostered new values of chivalry and respectable soldiering.

e. Building castles, fortresses, churches, and shrines throughout the Middle East to supply the crusaders and encourage religious pilgrimage advanced architectural technology and design.

These elements moved medieval society out of its narrow provincial European-centered perspective into a new age of culture, a renaissance. On the negative side, the crusades brought out the worst in European nobility and peasantry. Christian nations were ruthless in warfare. Often, the Muslims treated their captives with more human dignity and respect than the Christian crusaders. Thus, the crusades should be viewed as unholy wars.

Exercise 51

The Crusades

Directions: Read about the medieval crusades, and answer the questions that follow.

The quick growth of Islam threatened to engulf Byzantium (Constantinople). Feeling threatened on all sides, the Eastern emperors fought a series of wars against the Muslims, Bulgars, and Armenians. The Seljuk Turks, however, proved to be too large a force, and the Eastern armies were defeated at the Battle of Namzikert (1071). Asia Minor was invaded and, as a result, the Eastern Empire was deprived of over half of its territory.

The Eastern Emperor Alexius Comnenus appealed to Pope Urban II for aid in defending the Christian faith against invasion and attack. The pope responded with a sermon at a convocation in Clermont, France, calling people to return control of the Holy Land to Christian forces. Deus Vult (God wills it) became the battle cry, and the Crusader movement began.

Note below the route taken to capture Jerusalem.

How many evils has religion caused!

—Lucretius

The Crusader movement combined the elements of a military expedition backed by the Church and a pilgrimage to the Holy Land. The papacy was prominently involved in the movement from the beginning. The pope issued incentives for participation; crusaders were immune from taxes; crusaders' families and property were protected; indulgences guaranteed the crusaders' entry into heaven and reduced time in purgatory. The popes financed the operations and provided means of transportation to areas under siege.

Reflect:

1. Can the Crusader movement be justified in view of Jesus' teachings?

2. In what areas of the world is the crusader mentality still in operation?

3. What other ways exist to deal with conflict?

Crusader Quiz

Directions: Place the letter of the person or term which most appropriately corresponds to the description.

a. Urban II

b. Peter the Hermit

c. Outremer

d. Saracens

e. Knightly Orders

1. _____ Relayed a message to Europe concerning the fall of Jerusalem into Muslim hands, which started the first crusade movement

2. _____ Pope who called Europe to arms by starting the first crusade in 1095

3. _____ Eastern Christians' name for the Muslim Turks

4. _____ "Land beyond the sea," named for the collection of four Western Christian states set up in the Holy Land after the first crusade

5. _____ Hospitalors, Templars, Teutonic, Maltese Cross, all organizations of soldier-monks

6. _____ Leader of the "people's crusade" which was massacred in Asia Minor

Cathedrals

Directions: Research the following information about cathedrals. Some excellent resource materials are *Cathedral* by David Macaulay or *The Gothic Cathedral* by Otto von Simson. The information can be found in other sources as well.

1. Cathedral comes for the Latin word_____which means
   _____ .

2. What is the function of a cathedral? _____
   _____

3. In what ways is the cathedral the focus of city life?_____
   _____

4. How was the building of a cathedral financed? _____
   _____

5. Label the parts of the cathedral.

   a.

   b.

   c.

   d.

   e.

6. Romanesque style

      a. Walls were _____

      b. Windows were _____

      c. Arches were _____

   Gothic Style

      a. Walls were _____

      b. Windows were _____

      c. Arches were _____

7. What is on the western portal of all cathedrals?_____
   _____

8. How are relics related to cathedrals? _____
   _____

I never weary of great churches. It is my favourite kind of mountain scenery. Mankind was never so happily inspired as when it made a cathedral.

—Stevenson

105

9. What is the purpose of gargoyles? _____

    _____

10. What was the purpose of the cathedral chapter? _____

    _____

11. What is the function of the floor maze? _____

    _____

12. Why are the windows considered to be three dimensional books of
    instruction? _____

    _____

13. Why are so many cathedrals dedicated to Mary? _____

    _____

    _____

14. What is the purpose of flying buttresses? _____

    _____

Summary

1. Why did the building of a cathedral take so many years?

2. The cathedrals were built with a unity of purpose.
    What does this statement mean?

106

Return to the Gospel

Directions: Read about two founders of Mendicant orders below.

The cities of the twelfth and thirteenth centuries were fast becoming bustling places. Feudalism, which once thrived in rural areas, was dying. Invaders from the north no longer threatened populated areas, and the crusades reintroduced Greek and Muslim ideas to the universities in European cities. These events led to the growth of a new group in the cities, the middle class, which became involved in commerce, shopkeeping, and the new business of banking. In addition, great masses of the poor and sick began to gather around the walls of medieval cities.

As society changed, the old religious customs fell into disuse. Traditional monasticism had developed under the Benedictines and was reformed later by the Augustinian canons, the Cluniac and Cistercian monks, and the Premonstratensians. Despite all this, traditional monks did not relate well to the people of the cities, and the Church was in danger of getting out of touch with the times. Fortunately, two extraordinary people answered God's call to help the Church become more relevant to the urban cultures of the high Middle Ages.

John Bernardone (1182–1226) was the son of a prosperous cloth merchant in Italy. He was the pride of his family and the acknowledged leader of the young people of his hometown. There was no reason to doubt that John would become a wealthy, well-respected, popular citizen of Assisi, Italy.

God had other plans. The world knows and loves this man as St. Francis of Assisi. Francis ("The Frenchman") was a nickname given him early in life because he was fascinated by French culture and customs introduced to him by the travels of his father.

Along with other young people of Assisi, he went to war against a neighboring rival city. When he returned home ill, Francis underwent a profound conversion experience. Many people of the town thought he had gone insane, as he began giving away all his clothing and riches; he even gave away cloth from his father's warehouse. Francis had experienced, in the depth of his being, Jesus of the Gospels. From then on, his goal was to live Jesus' way of life. He began to devote his life to healing and serving the poor and sick, to preaching joy and hope to the despairing, and to respect for all of God's gifts of nature. His simplicity also found expression in his creation and display of the first Christmas crib scene.

Lord, make me an instrument of thy peace.

—St. Francis of Assisi

He later had another experience in which he was told by God, "Rebuild my church." Francis interpreted this to mean that he should literally repair the fallen down ruins of a small church near Assisi. What he did not realize then was that this call referred to the Church of God's people as well. The new religious order he founded, the Friars Minor (little brothers), more popularly known as the Franciscans, became the vanguard of a revitalized Church adapting to the currents of change taking place in the cities. The Church began again to be in touch with the middle class and urban poor.

With his friend, St. Clare, Francis founded a religious order for women called the Poor Clares. Another group, the third order consisted of lay people who did not take traditional vows but assisted the Franciscans in their work.

Another notable person who founded an order of friars was Dominic de Guzman (1170–1221), son of a noble Spanish family. He became a priest and was sent to southern France. He was shocked to discover the inroads made by the Albigensians. He was also scandalized by the worldly lives, ignorance, and poor example of the clergy of the region. He realized why the Church was losing the battle against this heresy and decided to combat it at its root. He founded a religious order patterned after that of Francis. The main emphasis of his group, however, was preaching. The group was called the Order of Preachers (O.P.) or Dominicans. While they did not entirely succeed in southern France, they did make progress where older religious orders had failed. The Dominicans went on to become the great teachers of the medieval universities.

Both Francis and Dominic founded orders which became known as *mendicants* (beggars). The following charts indicate similarities and differences between the traditional monastic orders (*e.g.*, Benedictines) and the Mendicants.

Similarities
1. They took traditional monastic vows.
2. Their lives were dedicated to serving God.
3. Their lifestyle was community centered.
4. They wore clothing, called habits, which identified them.

Differences	
Monastic Orders	*Mendicants*
1. Withdrew from society; lived in rural areas	1. Lived with people in cities
2. Earned their own living; were self-sufficient	2. Lived by begging; depended on people
3. Gave service to others in the form of prayer, agricultural knowledge, preservation of books	3. Gave direct service to the poor, cared for the sick, widows, orphans
4. Stayed in monasteries	4. Moved from town to town

The Rule of St. Francis

Directions: Study basic elements of the Rule of St. Francis, then complete the exercise.

In 1210, Francis and eleven of his brothers went to Rome to obtain the Church's permission for their new order. In a dramatic scene, Francis appeared at the doorway of Pope Innocent III's papal throne room. The man dressed in rags and sandals looked very much out of place amidst the luxury of the papal court. Fortunately for the Church, Innocent, besides being a shrewd lawyer, was also a spiritual man. He recognized in this shabby person a man of faith, trying to live the Gospel of Jesus. He approved Francis's order and sent him away with his blessing.

Basic elements of the Franciscan rule include the following:

A. Friars are to own no property.

B. Obedience in following Christ is necessary even when painful.

C. Obedience to Christ's will is necessary even when hurt relationships result.

D. Friars must depend on the generosity of others.

E. No one is to be called leader because all the brothers are equal in the service they give.

F. It is a privilege to live and serve the rejected—the poor, weak, and sick.

G. Friars live without a natural family in exchange for eternal rewards.

H. Friars wear poor clothing.

This is the rule and way of life of the Brothers Minor: to observe the holy gospel of our Lord Jesus Christ, living in obedience, without personal belongings and in chastity.

—The Rule of St. Francis

110

The approved rule differed from traditional monastic rules; all its regulations were based on the Gospels. Below are some biblical quotations used to support Francis's rule. Match each quotation with a specific rule.

1. _____ He heard this and said, "Those who are well do not need a physician, but the sick do. Go and learn the meaning of the words, 'I desire mercy, not sacrifice.' I did not come to call the righteous but sinners." *Matthew 9:12–13*

2. _____ Whatever town you enter and they welcome you, eat what is set before you, . . . *Luke 10:8*

3. _____ Then Jesus said to his disciples, "Whoever wishes to come after me must deny himself, take up his cross, and follow me." *Matthew 16:24*

4. _____ Jesus said to him, "If you wish to be perfect, go, sell what you have and give to [the] poor, and you will have treasure in heaven. Then come, follow me." *Matthew 19:21*

5. _____ And everyone who has given up houses or brothers or sisters or father or mother or children or lands for the sake of my name will receive a hundred times more, and will inherit eternal life. *Matthew 19:29*

6. _____ "If anyone comes to me without hating his father and mother, wife and children, brothers and sisters, and even his own life, he cannot be my disciple." *Luke 14:26*

7. _____ Then what did you go out to see? Someone dressed in fine garments? Those who dress luxuriously and live sumptuously are found in royal palaces. *Luke 7:25*

8. _____ But Jesus summoned them and said, "You know that the rulers of the Gentiles lord it over them, and the great ones make their authority over them felt. But it shall not be so among you. Rather, whoever wishes to be great among you shall be your servant; whoever wishes to be first among you shall be your slave. *Matthew 20:25–27*

111

Classical Proofs

Directions: St. Thomas Aquinas's most famous work, *Summa Theologiae*, includes five arguments for the existence of God which start from an empirical knowledge of the physical world. Read the "proofs" below. Then answer the questions that follow.

Argument 1: Things in this world are always changing and moving. Someone had to begin the movement or change in the first place. God is the one first mover.

Argument 2: People did not create themselves; the world around us did not cause itself to be. People and things are the effects of what came before them. God is the efficient cause of all that is.

Argument 3: The people around us, the world in which we live, and life as we know it did not have to be exactly this way. All life is dependent on someone or something else for survival. Logically this points to the necessity of a being who depends on nothing or no one else, a being who *has* to be—God.

Argument 4: Some actions are better than others; some people lead more noble lives than others. This sense of gradation of goodness points to one being who is fully good, fully noble, the highest expression of all that is holy—God.

Argument 5: The world around us and the events of history illustrate a sense of order that could not exist through accident. All things, events and people come to one distinct end—the principle of finality. Universal order points out the necessity of an intelligent orderer of all things—God.

112

*I do
not seek to
understand
that I may
believe,
but I believe
that I may
understand:
for this
I also
believe,
that unless
I believe
I will not
understand.*

—St. Anselm

St. Thomas Aquinas argued for the existence of God as the Unmoved Mover, the First Cause, the Necessary One, the Ultimate Goodness, and the Universal Orderer.

1. Does it make sense to believe in God in this day and age? Back up your answer with sound reasoning.

2. Which of St. Thomas Aquinas's arguments makes the most sense to you? Which is the most difficult to understand? Why?

3. Is it really possible to prove the existence of God? Why or why not? Does a lack of proof make our faith any less important?

4. Why should our faith be reasonable? Why is it important to have some solid ground upon which to base our beliefs?

5. How can the use of reason and intelligence help us grow closer to God?

Sing, My Tongue

Thomas Aquinas said that the highest form of Christian life is not action or contemplation, but the ability to integrate the two.

—Richard Rohr, OFM

114

Directions: Knowing *about* God is not the same thing as *knowing* God. Ultimately, intelligence and reason must help us grow in our relationship with God or else they are useless.

The prayer below, attributed to St. Thomas Aquinas, is filled with theological teachings about the mystery of our redemption. Yet it also takes these teachings a step further by applying the insights to a personal response to God's revelation. The last stanza shows the depth of response to which we are called. The prayer is often sung at Eucharistic devotions.

Paraphrase the prayer in your own words, and then spend some time reflecting on the meaning of Eucharist in your life.

Sing my tongue, the Savior's glory
Of his flesh the mystery sing:
Of the blood all price exceeding,
Shed by our immortal King,
Destined for the world's redemption,
From a noble womb to spring.

Of a pure and spotless Virgin
Born for us on earth below,
He, as man with others conversing,
Stayed, the seeds of truth to sow;
Then he closed in solemn order
Wondrously His life of woe.

On the night of that last supper
Seated with his chosen band,
He, the pascal victim eating,
First fulfills the Law's command;
Then as food to all his people
Gives himself with his own hand.

Word made Flesh, the bread of nature
By His word to Flesh He turns;
Wine into His Blood He changes,
Although eye no change discerns.
While the minds seek truth earnestly.
Faith gives what the minds may spurn.

Down in adoration falling,
Lo! the sacred Host we hail;
Lo! o'er ancient forms departing,
newer rites of grace prevail;
Faith for all defects supplying
where the feeble senses fail.

Church and State Clash

Directions: Read the following information about the life of St. Thomas Becket.

A classic example of Church/State conflict in the Middle Ages is the story of King Henry II of England (1145–1189) and Thomas Becket, Archbishop of Canterbury. Henry was the great-grandson of William the Conqueror who crossed the English Channel from Normandy, defeated the Saxons, and began a reign emphasizing centralized control of the government by the king. Like William, Henry II was determined to maintain firm control of the restless English barons, who resented the intrusion of foreign Norman nobles. He assumed that he had the last word about anything that happened in England. He was a good administrator. In appearance, he was a hefty man with a square, reddish face. He loved riding and hunting; he was always on the move. Full of passion, he was also unpredictable and violent when angry.

Henry's one real friend in his court was Thomas Becket. Thomas, son of a middle class family of Norman descent, was recognized early for his intelligence. He eventually was noticed by the Archbishop of Canterbury, the most powerful Church official in England; Thomas became his assistant. When Henry II, at twenty-one, became king, the archbishop recommended Thomas as a candidate to become chancellor, the king's leading advisor. Thomas had an engaging personality and was eager to please. He loved hunting, riding, and pleasure as much as Henry; they became close friends.

When the Archbishop of Canterbury died, Henry decided that his friend, Thomas, would be the ideal replacement. He assumed that with his best friend as chancellor and Archbishop of Canterbury, the king's power was assured. Thomas, sensing the dilemma that was to come, opposed the move. He resigned as chancellor when pressured to accept the position of archbishop.

As Thomas took on new duties, he also went through a conversion experience. He began to live a life of rigorous self-discipline, service to the poor, and prayer. He also took his job of being Archbishop seriously and began to assert the Church's authority in opposition to the king's wishes.

Henry began to feel betrayed. The situation came to a head over the issue of whether a priest who is accused of a crime would be tried in a Church court or the king's court. Thomas refused to turn the priest over to Henry. Henry responded by laying a trap for Becket. He demanded that Thomas appear in court to answer charges that he had embezzled money while chancellor. Thomas defiantly appeared with the archbishop's cross (symbolizing his authority over the king);

115

Will no one rid me of this turbulent priest?

—Henry II

he then demanded that his case be heard by the pope. Before Henry could act to stop him, Thomas slipped away and sought the protection of the French king, Louis VII.

After several years of exile in France, the pope gave Becket the authority to order an interdict against England. (An interdict involves the closing of churches and the refusal of permission to celebrate sacraments, except Baptism, in a particular location.) Implied in the threat was also the possibility of excommunication for Henry. This was considered a most serious action and would have led to severe reduction of the king's authority over his subjects. To avoid the interdict, Henry allowed Thomas to return to Canterbury.

Thomas continued to assert his authority. Henry, emotionally unstable, was blind with rage. During a meal with his barons, he demanded in a fit of temper to know why no one would help him to get rid of Becket. The final scene was about to begin.

116

Murder in the Cathedral

Directions: Read the following excerpt from T.S. Eliot's play, *Murder in the Cathedral*. The place is Canterbury Cathedral; the date is December 29, 1170. The characters include three priests, three knights, and Thomas Becket. Thomas has just arrived at the church to celebrate Vespers, the traditional monastic prayer recited in late afternoon.

[In the cathedral, Thomas and Priests.]

Priests

Bar the door. Bar the door.

The door is barred.

We are safe. We are safe.

They dare not break in.

They cannot break in. They have not the force.

We are safe. We are safe.

Thomas

Unbar the doors! throw open the doors!

I will not have the house of prayer, the church of Christ,

The sanctuary, turned into a fortress.

The Church shall protect her own, in her own way, not

As oak and stone; stone and oak decay,

Give no stay, but the Church shall endure.

The church shall be open, even to our enemies. Open the door!

117

Priest

My Lord! these are not men, these come not as men come, but

Like maddened beasts. They come not like men, who

Respect the sanctuary, who kneel to the Body of Christ,

But like beasts. You would bar the door

Against the lion, the leopard, the wolf or the boar,

Why not more

Against beasts with the souls of damned men, against men

Who would damn themselves to beasts. My Lord! My Lord!

Thomas   *You think me reckless, desperate and mad.*

You argue by results, as this world does,

To settle if an act be good or bad.

You defer to the fact. For every life and every act

Consequence of good and evil can be shown.

And as in time results of many deeds are blended

So good and evil in the end become confounded.

It is not in time that my death shall be known;

It is out of time that my decision is taken

If you call that decision

To which my whole being gives entire consent.

I give my life

To the Law of God about the Law of Man.

Unbar the door! unbar the door!

We are not here to triumph by fighting, by stratagem,
        or by resistance,

Not to fight with beasts as men. We have fought the beast

And have conquered. We have only to conquer

Now, by suffering. This is the easier victory.

Now is the triumph of the Cross, now

Open the door! I command it. OPEN THE DOOR!

[The door is opened. The Knights enter, slightly tipsy.]

Priests   This way, my Lord! Quick. Up the stair. To the roof.

To the crypt. Quick. Come. Force him.

Knights   Where is Becket, the traitor to the King?

Where is Becket, the meddling priest?

Come down Daniel to the lions' den,

Come down Daniel for the mark of the beast.

From Monarchy to Reform

118

Are you washed in the blood of the Lamb?

    Are you marked with the mark of the beast?

Come down Daniel to the lions' den,

    Come down Daniel and join in the feast.

Where is Becket the Cheapside brat?

    Where is Becket the faithless priest?

Come down Daniel to the lions' den,

    Come down Daniel and join in the feast.

It is the just man who **Thomas**

Like a bold lion, should be without fear.

I am here.

No traitor to the King. I am a priest,

A Christian, saved by the blood of Christ,

Ready to suffer with my blood.

This is the sign of the Church always,

The sign of blood. Blood for blood.

His blood given to buy my life,

My blood given to pay for His death,

My death for His death.

Absolve all those you have excommunicated. **First Knight**

Resign the powers you have arrogated. **Second Knight**

Restore to the King the money you appropriated. **Third Knight**

Renew the obedience you have violated. **First Knight**

From Monarchy to Reform

Thomas	*For my Lord I am now ready to die,*
	That His Church may have peace and liberty.
	Do with me as you will, to your hurt and shame;
	But not of my people, in God's name,
	Whether layman or clerk, shall you touch.
	This I forbid.
Priests	Traitor! traitor! traitor!
Thomas	*You, Reginald, three times traitor you:*
	Traitor to me as my temporal vassal,
	Traitor to me as your spiritual lord,
	Traitor to God in desecrating His Church.
First Knight	No faith do I owe to a renegade,
	And what I owe shall now be paid.
Thomas	*Now to Almighty God, to the Blessed Mary ever*
	Virgin, to the blessed John the Baptist, the holy
	apostles Peter and Paul, to the blessed martyr
	Denys, and to all the Saints, I commend my
	cause and that of the Church.[1]

120

[1]T. S. Eliot, *Murder in the Cathedral*, (N.Y.: Harcourt, Brace, & World, Inc.),

A Martyr's Death

Directions: Becket's murder was described by a writer of the time. Read the account and answer the questions that follow.

Scarcely had he spoken when the wicked knight, fearing that he (Becket) would be rescued by the people and escape alive, leapt upon him and wounded the sacrificial lamb of God in the head, slicing off the top of the skull, where the sacred chrism had dedicated him to God, and by the same stroke he almost severed the arm of him who tells this story. For he, when other monks and clerks had fled, stood by the saintly arch-bishop and held his arms around him till the one he interposed was nearly severed . . .

Becket received a second blow on the head, but still he staunchly stood. At the third blow he fell on knees and elbows, offering himself a living sacrifice and murmuring, "For the Name of Jesus and the pro-tection of the Church I am ready to embrace death."

But the third knight (Richard Brito) inflicted a terrible wound on him as he lay prostate, dashing the sword against the pavement. The whole crown of the head was hacked off . . .

The fourth knight (Hugh of Morville) beat back any who tried to intervene, giving the others freedom and license to commit the crime. But the fifth, no knight, but that clerk who had entered with the knights, put his foot on the neck of the holy priest and (called) out to the others. 'Let us be off, knights. This fellow will rise no more.'[1]

1. If you were an average English person of this time, how would you react to the murder of Thomas? Why? What circumstances of his killing would cause particular concern?

2. Think about the issue of Henry's guilt in the murder of Thomas. Was the king responsible for this death? Why or why not?

3. How is the story an example of Church/State issues common in the Middle Ages? Explain why there were so many bitter arguments at that period of history. Compare this episode with others.

[1]David Ayerst and A.S.T. Fisher, *Records of Christianity, Vol. II* (New York: Harper and Row Publishers, Inc., 1977), 300.

Three Great Calamities

Directions: Read the following information about the great calamities of the Middle Ages.

From 1050 to 1300, Christian Europe expanded in an age of faith. Huge Gothic and Romanesque churches with bell towers rising up to 500 feet into the air, impressively portrayed in brick and mortar Christian belief. Papal supremacy had won the medieval power struggle with warring feudal lords. Canon (church) law developed to maintain order and structure throughout Christian Europe. Religious orders, monastic and mendicant, had developed into hundreds of organizations. These religious were concerned with the spiritual welfare of God's pilgrim people under the protective and directive eyes of the papacy. Kings and princes, theologians and professors, monks and mendicants, businessmen and commoners turned to the pope for his respected decision on temporal and spiritual disputes. However, in the fourteenth century, Church and papal authority was beset with three great calamities that led Christians to clamor for a new reformation.

Avignon Papacy
(1305–1378)

122

Since the death of St. Peter, the popes had always lived in Rome. Medieval Christianity referred to the pope as "the Vicar of St. Peter." Rome had become the center for Church and papal authority. But with the election in 1305 of Clement V, a French cardinal who was not even present at the Roman conclave, the papal residence changed. This new pope moved into a castle at Avignon, France, and for the next seventy-three years his successors lived there under the protection of French kings. Most of the cardinals were French, too. Catholics who were not French, especially Roman citizens, called this the "Babylonian Captivity," comparing the era to the exile of the Israelites in Babylon. Various saints including St. Bridget of Sweden and St. Catherine of Siena, tried to persuade the pope to return to Rome.

Responding to the pleas of the people and prompted by the Spirit-directed encouragement of St. Catherine of Siena, Pope Gregory XI moved the papacy back to Rome in 1378.

The Avignon popes were not inactive but used their ecclesiastical authority quite judiciously. They clamped down on the Spiritual Franciscans, who represented a movement that called for a lifestyle of extreme poverty. They employed Dominican friars to handle the business of bringing heretics to trial through the "Holy Inquisition."

John Wycliff and later, John Hus, the Bohemian priest, taught that the Church instituted by Christ was invisibly constituted in the hearts of the "redestined" faithful. Every Christian could read and interpret the Bible without need of papal or official Church authority.

Because of these teachings, the Council of Constance (1414–1418) condemned the reforming teachings of Wycliff and bore some responsibility for burning Hus at the stake as a heretic.

Only two months after returning to Rome from Avignon, Pope Gregory XI died. It took the cardinals almost a year to elect a new pope. The Roman people demanded an Italian pope and threatened harm to the cardinals if the election did not produce this. The new pope, Urban VI was an Italian. The dissatisfied French cardinals went home and elected their own "pope," Clement VII, who moved into the Avignon papal residence. The Church now seemed to have two popes at the same time. Various European countries began to line-up supporting either the Avignon or the Roman pope. Christian Europe was split; a Church schism complicated continental life.

The next thirty years saw scholars and clergy trying to reunite a divided Church. The times also prompted discussion about the rights and duties of authority. Rival popes made offers to meet one another and straighten things out. The meetings never happened.

University people presented theories and new ideas consistent with their views of theology and canon law to rectify the Western Schism. Conciliarism gave a general council representing the main bodies of the whole church power and authority over the divided papacy. This resulted in a "council" of Pisa that drew 500 representatives. They elected Alexander V as the new pope; they made a major mistake in not obtaining the resignations of the Avignon or Roman popes who promptly refused to step aside. Then the Church had three popes! Within a year, Alexander died and was replaced by "Pope" John XXIII. Western Christianity was in a worse state than it was before the Council of Pisa.

It took the council of Constance (1414–1418), one of the longest councils in history, to settle the Western Schism. Sigismund, the German Emperor, prevailed upon the Pisan "Pope" John XXIII to start the council process. During the ensuing years the Roman pope, Gregory XII, resigned. John XXIII was deposed, and the Avignon "Pope" Benedict XIII died. Finally, a new pope was elected. A good, holy man, Martin V (1417–1431), was to unify the Catholic Church again as the Roman pontiff; thus ended one of the darkest chapters in Church history.

The Western Schism (1378-1417)

123

Consciousness of the past alone can make us understand the present.

—Herbert Luethy

The Black Death
(1348-1350)

The third great calamity of this age affected every man, woman, and child of medieval society. This was a plague that consisted of bubonic, septicemic, and pneumatic sicknesses spread by fleas carried by rats from merchant ships. No emperor, king, prince, pope, or bishop could stop it, and many fell victim to it. History calls it the Black Death—the great plague. Early in 1348, a merchant ship was washed ashore in southern Europe with its entire crew diseased and bloated. The disease quickly spread, first through Italy, then through southern France, Spain, and the Rhineland/Bavarian regions. No European country escaped it. It claimed victims regardless of position or social rank.

Once infected, a person suffered bleeding under the skin and turned a darkened color. The disease induced vomiting, coughing, diarrhea, and usually death within twelve hours. No known medical treatment could stop its march. Doctors and clergymen were especially susceptible as they attempted to bring treatment and comfort to the victims. Within two years, one quarter to one-third of the entire population of Europe died. Two-thirds of the clergy were wiped out. In England alone the population dropped from 3,700,000 in 1347 to below 2,000,000 by 1400. It is estimated that forty million people in Europe succumbed to this pestilence.

The plague brought about economic hardships as well. Fields were untended, merchants' shops were deserted, and trade routes to the East were less travelled. Commerce slowed to a virtual standstill. The Christian population pleaded to the Almighty for divine intervention. Churches and shrines were filled with people begging for a miracle. When none came, the spiritual life of many people waned. Although the plague finally died out, long-term spiritual effects were to manifest themselves over the next two centuries.

The Avignon Papacy

Part A

Directions: The Western Schism generated a situation in which "popes" resided in Avignon, Pisa, and Rome. Using **Exercise 61** for information, write the name of each pope under the appropriate place of his residence.

Avignon Popes	Roman Popes	Pisan Popes
1.	1.	1.
2.	2.	2.
3.	3.	
4.	4.	

Part B

Directions: Fill in the blank with the term that most appropriately fits the context.

People came to call the Avignon Papacy the (1)_____ because it corresponded to ancient Israel's exile from 587–539 B.C. Yet, the Avignon popes remained active as they settled many Church controversies including the disagreement with the (2)_____ _____over the poverty of Christ. Later on, in order to solve the problem of more than one pope, the university people developed the concept of (3)_____which gave a council limited powers over the papacy. Meanwhile, the rest of medieval society was suffering a sweeping plague called the (4)_____ _____.

Part C

Directions: Explain briefly the role played by each of the following during the period of the three medieval calamities.

1. St. Catherine of Siena

2. Council of Pisa

3. University scholars

4. Council of Constance

5. Sigismund, the Roman Emperor

Persecution has not crushed it, power has not beaten it back, time has not abated its force, and, what is most wonderful of all, the abuses and treasons of its friends have not shaken its stability.

—Horace Bushnell

125

Face the Church

> *We should not attach much value to what we have given God, since we shall receive for the little we have bestowed much more in this life and in the next.*
>
> *—St. Teresa of Avila*

Directions: Read the following imaginary dialogues with three great saints.

Hill   Greetings everyone! I'm your host, Pete Hill, and today on *Face the Church* we will present an interview with those of the greatest woman saints of all time: Catherine of Siena, Joan of Arc, and Teresa of Avila. Ms. Arc is tied up with some legal proceedings at the moment, so we will begin our conversation with Catherine, who comes from a rather large family.

Catherine   *Yes, Pete, I am the youngest of twenty-four children, and my father adopted one boy during the plague of 1348. Unfortunately, almost half of my brothers and sisters died in infancy. My father was a wood dyer in Siena. He also owned a farm and a vineyard next to our home. He was a great person—fair and honest with his workers, kind and generous to his family, humble and loving before God. He was active in politics and gave that interest to the family as well. In fact, my brother Bartolomeo was once elected one of the twelve rulers of the City of Siena. My mother, however, was a real character. Her number one passion in life was to get all her daughters married and all her sons settled in business as early as possible. Whatever didn't fit into these plans, she considered to be unimportant.*

Hill   Didn't you want to get married?

Catherine   *Not at age thirteen! The more my mother tried to marry me off the less I wanted it to happen. She began dressing me up and styling my hair. She refused to let me go outside by myself and began parading me in front of every eligible young man in the city. Then when I was sixteen, my sister Bonaventura died unexpectedly. I was so close to her! One day, while I was still grieving over her loss, my parents started discussing in detail all of the advantages of my prospective suitor. I was furious and announced once and for all that I would never be married. They dragged me off to see this priest who said that if I wasn't going to get married, then I had to be a nun. I told him that was nonsense, I had no intention of being a nun. After all, what's wrong with being single? He said that I would be an old maid and that people would laugh at me. But I didn't care. It would have been unfair to force me into a lifestyle I didn't want. So, after a lot of discussion and pulling strings I was able to join the Third Order of St. Dominic, a secular order of lay people who follow Dominican spirituality.*

When did you first realize that you were different from other children?	**Hill**

When I was about six, my brother Stefano and I were walking home from Bonaventura's house. Suddenly—I know it sounds strange—I had this vision of Christ looking at me lovingly. I was stunned and felt overwhelmed by what I saw. God loved me! Me, little Catherine! God thought I was special. It changed my life. I needed time to think, pray, and sort out my feelings. — *Catherine*

At six?!	**Hill**

I grew up fast. You would have to with as many brothers and sisters as I had. Surely there have been times when you, too, Pete, had to be wise beyond your years. I just wanted to grow closer to Christ. — *Catherine*

How did you do that?	**Hill**

I fasted and prayed. I learned to read Scripture even though the people of my day did not approve of women learning anything at all. I worked in the hospital for a while and took care of lepers and plague victims. I even buried them after they died. Nobody else would come near them, but I knew they needed love, human touch, and compassion. — *Catherine*

127

Some say your ascetic practices were carried too far: eating and drinking a minimum of food; for a while consuming only the communion host; sleeping on a board for just an hour every night.	**Hill**

A lot of people don't understand fasting these days. I did it to show that I had control over my body and passions. Wars, family rivalries, and complicated politics put Italy and France in a mess. Through my acts of self-control, I hoped others would follow suit and end the fighting. I offered God my pain as a prayer for peace. It worked, too! — *Catherine*

Catherine, how did you become involved in politics?	**Hill**

Understand please, that for the better part of the fourteenth century, the popes resided in France and, unfortunately, followed the will of the French king. I was firmly convinced that all of the riots in Rome and the wars in France were because of the pope not residing in Rome where he belonged. I undertook a letter-writing campaign to get Pope Gregory XI to return to Rome. I think I shocked him, though; I told him to stand up, be a man, quit complaining, and go back to Rome where he belonged! He did. After he died, the cardinals elected Urban VI, who tried to reform the Church. The French bishops, who had prestigious jobs under the French popes, got upset and elected their own pope. I spent the rest of my life trying to get the whole Church to recognize Pope Urban VI. — *Catherine*

From Monarchy to Reform

Hill	I see that Joan of Arc has just arrived from Rouen. How goes the trial, Joan?
Joan	*Not very well, I'm afraid. Everyone keeps twisting my words around. They are out to prove that I'm a witch.*
Hill	Do they have any proof?
Joan	*Not as far as I'm concerned. But they are using my clothing, my actions, and my voices as proof.*
Hill	Let's face it, Joan. Cutting your hair and dressing like a man are not normal behavior for a nineteen-year-old peasant girl.
Joan	*Have you ever tried to ride a horse while wearing a dress? Take it from me, it is rather difficult, not to mention painful and immodest. Wearing men's clothing was a practical way to get a job done.*
Hill	What was that job?
Joan	*To help unify France by driving the Burgundians out of town and to make sure that the Dauphin was crowned as King Charles VII.*
Hill	A woman—going to do all of this?
Joan	*Well, somebody had to get the troops going and lead them to victory. The Dauphin certainly wasn't going to do it.*
Hill	But why you?
Joan	*Why not? God often uses the small and the weak to accomplish his will. Maybe God told lots of people to lead the troops; the difference is that I listened.*
Hill	You had divine help in your military accomplishments?
Joan	*The voices told me what needed to be done, but the troops needed to be rallied for a cause. I was able to unify them, give them a sense of direction, and a cause for which to fight. I got them to pray together and to rely upon one another and God.*

128

Did you like the fighting? Was it exciting for you?	**Hill**

I hated it. Such a cruel and senseless waste of life! I used to write to the opposition, tell them what I was going to do, and beg them to leave the city before the fighting started. I wanted to avoid war at all cost. But fighting was always the last resort. There were times, in the midst of battle, when I would get off of my horse and hold the hand of a dying soldier so he wouldn't have to face that moment alone. It didn't matter which side he was on. Everybody deserves comfort on a deathbed. — ***Joan***

Weren't you afraid that you would be killed, too?	**Hill**

There are worse things in life than dying for what you believe in. I was wounded a few times, but I recovered. — ***Joan***

What is the present status of your trial?	**Hill**

As you know, I was captured by the English and deported. I am standing trial for witchcraft. It is strange, but Charles VII has made no attempt to come to my defense. I am a little disappointed in him for that. — ***Joan***

How are you spending your time in jail?	**Hill**

They won't let me go to Mass or Communion. I spend my time sewing, weaving, and doing needlepoint. If I ever get out of there I will be able to use these things to set up housekeeping. — ***Joan***

Do you want a family of your own, Joan?	**Hill**

Isn't that every young girl's dream? To be honest, though, I don't expect to get out alive. I will have to make do with Jesus and Mary being my family. — ***Joan***

What will happen if you are found guilty?	**Hill**

I will be burned at the stake. But you know, I can't go against my conscience and what I believe God told me to do. I know that if I remain faithful, even if I die, I will live eternally with Jesus. They can kill my body but never my spirit. — ***Joan***

129

Hill	We turn now to Teresa of Avila, who has taken a moment from her busy schedule to speak with us today. Teresa, what are you doing these days?
Teresa	*I've been traveling throughout Spain setting up convents and monasteries and trying to reform the religious order I belong to—the Carmelites.*
Hill	Why do they need to be reformed?
Teresa	*Conditions in the Spanish Monasteries have become positively scandalous! There's been a relaxation of our traditional disciplines and vows. It has gotten to the point in some places that monastic life is extremely luxurious. This is not the type of lifestyle Antony, Pachomius, and the founding Fathers had in mind when they described the daily martyrdom of a monastic.*
Hill	It sounds like you are down on money and luxury.
Teresa	*I don't have a problem with people having money. I couldn't have founded St. Joseph's convent without the financial support of my wealthy relatives and friends. I do have a problem with money being the consuming passion of a group of people who are supposed to be working on ways of controlling their passions. Surely, there is still room for sacrifice and simplicity of lifestyle even in this day and age!*
Hill	I understand that you've become quite an author, Teresa. I've read some of your books—your *Autobiography*, the *Interior Castle* and *The Way of Perfection*. If you don't mind me saying so, sometimes they seem a bit strange—almost sensual and erotic. Care to comment?
Teresa	*People call me a mystic. That's just a fancy term for someone whose entire being—body, mind, heart, and soul—is united completely to God in love. Of course that's sensual! I feel God's presence in my life; I love God totally and completely, with every ounce of my being. I get dizzy just thinking about how it feels to love God so completely. More importantly, God loves me totally and completely. Haven't you ever been in love, Pete? Don't you know that feeling? Sometimes people think you're high; and I guess you are, in a most natural and drug-free way.*

130

Describe for us your ideas about prayer.	**Hill**

In my book, The Interior Castle, *I use symbolic imagery to describe seven rooms or stages in our souls. As we travel through these "rooms," we grow deeper into prayer. The first few rooms deal with purging from ourselves all that distracts us from total union with God. After dealing with our fears and distractions to prayer, we must quiet ourselves and then unite ourselves to God—totally and completely. I use the images of a betrothal and a white butterfly to explore the dynamics of the prayer life. Then the last few "rooms" deal with feelings of desolation, which occur in the best of relationships, and "spiritual marriage," in which the soul is in a permanent state of union with God.*	*Teresa*

It sounds like your entire life is devoted to prayer and contemplation.	**Hill**

It is, but I must admit that sometimes it gets difficult to balance prayer with my work in reforming the Carmelite order. But I guess that when your heart is united to God, then everything you do is a prayer, too.	*Teresa*

That's all the time we have. Thank you Catherine of Siena, Joan of Arc and Teresa of Avila for your insights. Join us next week for another edition of *Face the Church.*	**Hill**

Reflections

Directions: Answer the following questions.

1. Catherine of Siena believed that all Christians—especially the laity—had a responsibility to leadership within the Church. What, in your opinion, can you do to make the Church a better institution?

2. Joan of Arc would have escaped martyrdom if she had denounced her actions and her belief in God. Is there anything for which you would have the courage to put your life on the line?

3. Teresa of Avila balanced a hectic work schedule with a deep like of contemplative prayer. How do you go about striking this balance in your own life?

> *A hero gives the illusion of surpassing humanity. The saint doesn't surpass it, but assumes it, and strives to realize it in the best possible way.*
>
> —Georges Bernanos

132

Part **4**

From Luther to Trent

I pray not only for them, but also for those who will believe in me through their word, so that they may all be one, as you, Father, are in me and I in you, that they also may be in us, that the world may believe that you sent me.

—John 17:20–21

There have been a number of times in the Church's history when reform was needed. The growth of heresies indicated a need for reform. Movements like monasticism helped bring positive changes in the church. In the sixteenth century, the Church again found itself in need of change. This time it failed to react in time, and the Church became badly divided.

Why?

There are a number of reasons. Luther, Calvin, Zwingli and other reformers became influential. The clergy were in disarray, and poor education of priests led to abuses. People had been disappointed by papal behavior during the Avignon papacy and the Western Schism.

These events led to a lessening of the prestige of the popes. With the scandalous lifestyle of many of the Renaissance popes, disaster resulted when the pope's authority was again challenged. Because of their worldliness and fear of losing power, popes allowed the Church to drift into chaos by responding sluggishly to pleas from reformers. The leaders compounded their error by not calling a council, a time-tested means of dealing with serious problems.

However, the popes alone were not to blame. Other factors were revolutionizing society itself. The medieval world was crumbling, and a new era was being born.

This period of time was called the Renaissance (rebirth). It received its name because of revived interest in the old Greco-Roman art and architecture. It had other characteristics, too: the new scientific method of studying the world was born; new forms of art and literature flourished; new respect for the material world and its beauty developed; emphasis on human beings as the most perfect creatures replaced emphasis on God and the afterlife; new inventions made their appearance. Leonardo da Vinci, the ultimate Renaissance man, even dreamed and planned a flying machine long before the Wright brothers. It was a time of new knowledge and ideas. Information could be quickly passed around because of the development of the printing press. Emphasis in society shifted from the importance of community effort to the importance of the individual and the development of the potential of each human being.

It was inevitable that in this renaissance climate, the Catholic Church, which so identified itself with medieval life and customs, would be badly shaken. That it survived the cataclysm of the Reformation can be seen as a fulfillment of Jesus' promise that he would be with the Church until the end of time. However, we still live in hope that someday we may again embody Jesus' prayer for unity. Through the action of the Holy Spirit, the Catholic Church survived. In the process it became smaller in number, but it also became a healthier Church.

From Luther to Trent

Causes of the Reformation

Directions: Study the following information about the Church during the Renaissance.

The decades which preceded the Reformation set the stage for desperately needed changes in the Church. A variety of factors paved the way to necessary reforms.

a. *Philosophy and Education*

The great schools and universities which sprang up during the thirteenth and fourteenth centuries were educating more lay-men than clergy during the Renaissance. Through studying the ancient philosophers, educated laymen began to realize that "the proper study of mankind is man." While the Church's spiritual influence was deteriorating due to poorly trained and uneducated clergy, these well-educated laymen asserted fresh ideas and insights into the nature of humanity. A new philosophy called *humanism* developed. Men such as Thomas More and Erasmus, deeply concerned about the quality of life for all, exercised tremendous influence on civil rulers and Church officials alike.

These humanists were anticlerical but not antireligious. They were appalled to go to Mass and experience a poorly trained, semi-illiterate priest stumbling over the Latin prayers and preaching inadequately. How could the Gospel of Christ Jesus be understood by the common Christian if it was poorly preached? Humanists clamored for change, reforms, and spiritual renewal.

b. *Liturgy*

In Rome, papal ceremonies were celebrated with formal pageantry lasting for hours. In some small towns, Masses were celebrated with irreverent haste. In both cases, the spiritual dimensions of the meaning of the Eucharist were lost. Holy Communion was only offered to commoners a few times a year; this was a setting for spiritual malnourishment. Eucharistic piety centered on devotions to the Blessed Sacrament outside of Mass. Anyone could go to a church any time to be in the presence of the Eucharist and simply adore for hours. Churches also provided special devotions to the Blessed Mother, the Precious Blood of Jesus, and to the thousands of saints whose relics had been brought to Europe by the crusaders. Veneration of relics and devotional cults to saints were primary means for many Christians in the practice of their faith. The focus and importance of the Mass and Scripture were lost.

> *I wish that the Scriptures might be translated into all languages, so that not only the Scots and the Irish, but also the Turks and the Saracens might read and understand them. I long that the farm-labourer might sing them as he follows his plough, the weaver hum them to the tune of his shuttle, the traveller beguile the weariness of his journey with their stories.*
>
> —*Erasmus*

c. *Clerical Abuses*

The upper hierarchy (cardinals and bishops) became secularized. These men lost the sense of spiritual mission which was the main reason for their ministry. Some were as incapable of teaching as the least of their uneducated clergy. Greed set in as well. Bishops were often chosen by the nobility with papal blessing. Two types arose to episcopal office: relatives of the nobels and upper clergy; people who could afford to buy favors which led to office (simony). Popes allowed this practice for a price. A bishop could be appointed over more than one diocese. Some dioceses produced more income than others; this created the situation of absentee bishops in low income producing dioceses. The diocese of Milan, for instance, did not receive a bishop's visit for 100 years!

Lesser clergy were poorly trained, poorly financed, and poorly supervised. Many had little or no knowledge of Church teaching or the sacraments. There was no formal education to prepare for clerical duties. Bishops, more concerned with temporal pursuits, were apathetic about education for priests.

d. *The Renaissance Popes*

The popes of the late 1400s and early 1500s were among the wealthiest men of their age. Simony, concubination (having mistresses), political power-brokerage, and nepotism (appointing relatives to ecclesiastical office) were sins openly practiced by men in the papal office. This age produced more unworthy popes than any other. Yet, God's grace works through human instruments in spite of their weaknesses. Many of these popes made lasting and positive contributions to the Church despite their personal inadequacies.

e. *Indulgence Problems*

The Church's doctrine on indulgences stated that even after one confessed sin there was temporal punishment for the sin which one would suffer in purgatory after one's death. However, certain acts and objects had the power to remit all or part of the punishment. An indulgence would take away all or part of the punishment. During the crusades, soldiers gained such indulgences by fighting on military pilgrimages. Those who supported them financially also gained indulgences granted by the papal office.

Due to the expense of constructing St. Peter's Basilica and luxurious papal expenditures, Rome was in need of some quick cash. Solution: Issuing the sale of new indulgences. A cleverly gifted Dominican friar, Johann Tetzel was commissioned as the papal salesman. Every good salesman has a gimmick, and indulgences were difficult theological products to sell to commoners who knew nothing of theology. Tetzel's gimmick was a sales pitch worthy of a modern advertising agency:

> When a coin in the coffer rings
> a soul from purgatory springs.

The meaning was clear; the sooner one paid for the papal indulgence, the quicker souls of deceased relatives would spring out of the fires of purgatory into heaven. With the aid of the new Guttenburg printing press the advertising campaign was begun. Common Christians, anxious to appease God, quickly lined-up with coins to buy salvation.

How Reforms Happen

Directions: Read the following information about the Church's ways of reforming itself.

The Church is made of human beings who strive together to remain faithful to the teachings of Jesus Christ. Try as we might, we sometimes stumble on the path of faith. And yet, the Church is called to be perfect (*Matthew 5:48*). When the Church finds itself in need of reform, it is obligated to reconcile itself to the Gospel message.

Several people and offices are used to aid the Church in following the right path. First and foremost, change and renewal usually begin as a grass roots effort. The whole people of God are called to the life of faith. This requires ongoing conversion to follow Christ more fully. Once conversion happens on an individual level, institutional change is more likely to occur. This is where the special ministry of the pope and bishops enters. They are charged with shepherding the Church community to remain faithful to the teachings of Christ.

Theologians, too, have a role in this process. Theologians help to interpret the meaning of the Church's teachings. They also ask questions that need to be asked regarding where the Church is headed in the future. Many times their work is speculative in nature; sometimes it does not hold up to close scrutiny. However, theologians can bring to light new and exciting insights about Scripture, the Church, and the Christian life.

Working together through dialogue and meeting together regularly, Church leaders guide the pilgrim Church on the path of faith. Church Councils are meetings of the entire hierarchy to examine problems or to set new directions for the community. Synods are bi-annual meetings of bishops to discuss specific issues concerning the Church. The bishops of a particular country meet regularly to deal with topics of concern to their specific locale. For example, the United States Bishops have met to discuss the economy and the challenge of peace.

The Church makes known its reforms in a variety of ways. Encyclicals are papal letters to the universal Church explaining how the Church is to respond to a specific issue. Pastoral letters, issued by bishops, also treat specific concerns such as the Church's attitudes toward sexuality and social justice.

Where understanding and desire end, there is darkness, and there God shines.

—Meister Eckhart

138

For Research:

1. Determine when the last Church council took place.
    Where was it held? What issues did it cover? Who called it?

2. Determine when the last bishops' synod took place.
    Where was it held? What issues did it cover? Who called it?

3. Determine when the last meeting of the National Conference
    of Catholic Bishops took place. What issues were discussed
    at the meeting? Who is president of the Conference?

The Splintering of Christianity

Directions: Read the following information about Martin Luther's break with the Church.

On October 31, 1517, when Martin Luther hammered up a notice of topics for debate on a church door in Wittenburg, Germany, he was doing something very ordinary for a university town of the sixteenth century. What he did not know was that his posting of the ninety-five theses would be the start of a religious revolution. The aftershocks are still affecting Christianity; the reformation had begun.

Luther never intended to found a new religion. In fact, the division of Christianity which resulted from his action was always a source of sorrow to him. He was neither a supporter of social reform or a champion of individual rights. His burning desire was to reform a Church he saw as having been corrupted by evil practices. He felt, in conscience, an obligation to correct them.

Luther grew up as a promising child in a miner's family. His father was stern and exacting. Young Martin dropped out of law school to become an Augustinian monk after nearly being struck by lightning. Interpreting his survival as a sign from God, he made a vow to enter monastic life.

Luther became an ideal monk—too ideal. While earning a doctor of theology degree and teaching at the University of Wittenberg, Luther was driven to be perfect. However, no matter how severe the discipline and penances he demanded of himself, he could not shake off the tremendous guilt he felt before a God he considered very judgmental. He nearly despaired of ever pleasing the God he loved and wished would love him back.

One day, while praying in his monk's cell overlooking the city, Luther was reading Paul's Epistle to the Romans. He had read these passages many times before. This time, though, one verse suddenly held new meaning for him:

For I am not ashamed of the gospel. It is the power of God for the salvation of everyone who believes: . . . "The one who is righteous by faith will live."
—*Romans 1:16–17*

For the first time that he could remember, Luther experienced freedom from the terrible burden of guilt. From this personal event, referred to as the *tower experience*, was to develop the most important of Luther's beliefs—justification by faith alone: nothing a person does can earn any favor with God; salvation comes as a free gift of grace from God and is totally unearned by anything a person does.

This belief which prompted his posting of the ninety-five theses, was a direct challenge to the preaching of indulgences as it was prac-

Good works do not make a man good, but a good man does good works.

—Martin Luther

From Luther to Trent

ticed at the time. Although the Catholic Church never taught that people could buy their way into heaven with indulgences, preachers such as the Dominican Johann Tetzel gave people that idea. Luther registered a complaint about Tetzel's behavior with the Archbishop of Mainz, the territory where Tetzel was preaching. The archbishop was dependent on indulgence income to bail himself out of debt, and Rome had agreed to let him keep half of the proceeds from sales in his area. Rather than calling a halt to the abuses, he sent a complaint to Rome about Luther's challenge. The Dominicans, too, conservatives of their day, joined against Luther. He began to accumulate powerful enemies.

A debate in Leipzig with the Dominican Johann Eck, a grueling affair for Luther, lasted eleven days. Eck cornered Luther into denying the pope's supremacy over the Church. It is interesting to note that Pope Leo X didn't seem to care; he was too concerned with hunting and other pleasures to worry very much about an obscure German monk.

As threats continued, Luther became more radical. In 1520 he produced three works, further developing his ideas. He attacked rituals and good works, stressing the importance of a personal relationship with God. He rejected all the sacraments except Baptism and Eucharist; priesthood was for all believers, not just for an ordained clergy. He fought the concepts of pilgrimages, relics, honoring of saints, friars, and priestly celibacy. He claimed that the papacy was a purely human invention with no divine authority. The Bible alone was to be the basis of Protestant Christianity.

No longer able to ignore the gathering storm, Pope Leo X issued a declaration that Luther had sixty days to change his mind or be excommunicated as a heretic. It was too late for a reconciliation. On the sixtieth day, Luther publicly burned the pope's demands, acting out his defiance of papal authority.

The final break with the Catholic Church occurred at a meeting called by the Holy Roman Emperor Charles V in the German city of Worms. At this meeting Luther was questioned publicly by the emperor. Luther stated, "I am bound by the Scriptures I have quoted and my conscience is captive to the Word of God. I cannot and I will not retract anything, since it is neither safe nor right to go against conscience . . . May God help me. Amen."

In his remaining twenty-five years. Luther married and had six children. (He also had a dog named Blockhead!) Luther translated the entire Bible into German; he also wrote many hymns, numerous devotional books, and two catechisms.

After Luther's death in 1546, Europe endured one-hundred years of bitter religious wars. The resulting geographical divisions along religious lines still exist. What began as a movement to correct abuses turned into the questioning of many doctrines, a reorganization of churches based on biblical authority and individual conscience, and the division of Christianity into many denominations.

Martin's Maze

Directions: Use the clues given to complete the crossword puzzle.

Across

3. At the Diet of _____ Luther finalized his break with the Catholic Church.

8. The belief that God's grace alone saves us is called _____ by faith.

10. A _____ is a book of questions and answers used to teach the beliefs of a religion.

11. Luther participated in an eleven day debate in _____ .

12. As a young man, Luther felt tremendous _____ before a judgmental God.

15. Luther had a dog named _____ .

17. The Reformation began when Luther posted the ninety-five _____.

Down

1. Pope _____ X excommunicated Luther.

2. When he read Paul's Epistle to the _____ , Luther had a religious experience.

4. Luther _____ the pope's letter of excommunication.

5. Luther left law school to become an _____ monk.

6. "The _____ Alone!" became the basis of Protestant belief.

7. One sacrament not rejected by Luther was _____ .

9. Johann _____ debated with Luther and got him to deny the pope's supremacy.

13. After Luther's death, Europe was torn by _____ wars for 100 years.

14. The second sacrament not rejected by Luther was _____ .

16. Johann _____ was an indulgence preacher in Germany.

Swiss Herald News

1550–1600 Edition   ☆☆☆☆☆   ☆☆☆☆☆   3¢

Calvinism Branches Out

The Swiss reform, acting independently from the Lutheran movement, has divided into three distinct branches. In France, long the site of many wars, the Calvinists are known as Huguenots; in Scotland, under the direction of John Knox, the religion is known as Presbyterianism; and in England the movement is called Puritanism.

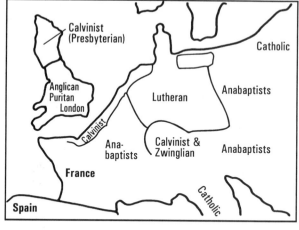

Former Slave Reforms Scotland

John Knox, a former galley slave, has succeeded in bringing the reform movement to Scotland. A student of John Calvin in Geneva, Switzerland, Knox returned to Scotland in 1559 to begin writing his book, *Confession of Faith*, in which he speaks out against the papacy, Mass, and Catholic idolatry. Mary Queen of Scots has opposed Knox's teachings from the outset because of his brutal attacks against Catholicism. The Queen is now in prison and is expected to be beheaded soon.

St. Bartholomew's Day Massacre

(Paris, 1572) A Calvinist congregation in France was destroyed last night in a bloody massacre. The people of France have been staunch supporters of Catholicism and have resisted all attempts at reform. The people claim that the Calvinist reform is politically motivated and is the source of many civil wars within the nation.

Weather:
Hot today, with a chance of avalanches in the upper parts of the Alps.

Traveller's Forecast:
Unseasonably mild weather is expected in Scotland for the golfing tournament.

Lottery Numbers:
7, 12, 19, 22, 27, 36

———— advertisement ————

Gutenburg Bible now available in Swiss, German, and English. Order your copy today.

144

Protestant Hopes Run High

King Henry IV, a Protestant, ascended to the throne today and is expected to lead reform movements in France. French Catholics are threatening to form an alliance with the King of Spain to wage war against his royal highness unless he converts to Catholicism. It is unknown whether Henry IV will yield for the sake of peace or risk war for his religious practices.

Marburg Debate Scheduled

Martin Luther, a German reformer, and Ulrich Zwingli of Zurich, Switzerland are scheduled to debate the nature of Eucharist this Saturday. Luther rejects Zwingli's idea that the sacrament is merely a symbol of Christ's presence but also warns against the magical belief in the real presence of Christ in the sacrament.

Protestants and Catholics Unite to End Anabaptism

In an historic and unprecedented move, Catholic and Protestant Churches are uniting to stamp out the practice of Anabaptism. Yesterday in Munster, Westphalia, thousands of Anabaptists were put to death for illegal and heretical teachings. The anabaptists (re-baptizers) are viewed as modern day Donatists by the Catholic forces and as a threat to the "faith alone" teachings of all reformed churches. Toleration of the sect has diminished lately and more persecutions are expected soon.

Who Are the Anabaptists?

The Anabaptists are the fastest growing protestant group to date. They are composed of a loose grouping of various religious beliefs, all of which reject infant baptism in favor of adult baptism after a confession of faith. However, baptism is not the central issue for the Anabaptists. At question is their conviction regarding the role the civil government should play in the reformation of Christianity. The Anabaptists support the idea that a community of Christians, led by the Holy Spirit, should initiate scripture-backed reforms regardless of state backing. They believe that a Church should be separate and distinct from society, even if the society claims to be Christian.

Anabaptists see themselves as missionaries to people of lukewarm faith. Rather than stressing reform, they prefer a restoration of the vigor and faithfulness of the earliest Christian communities. They stress that a true Christian relationship with Jesus Christ must go beyond simple inner experience and acceptance of doctrines to include a daily walk with God. Their lifestyle reflects Christian conversion.

Anabaptists reject the swearing of oaths, are complete pacifists (refuse to go to war or defend selves against persecution), and believe in mutual aid and the redistribution of wealth. Some practice a form of Christian communism.

The Amish and Mennonite communities trace their beliefs to the Anabaptist practices.

Thank you St. Jude for favors granted.

C.M.J.

145

Edict of Nantes Grants Freedom of Worship

The question of King Henry IV's religious views was settled yesterday when he issued the Edict of Nantes to grant freedom to practice Reformed Christianity in France. Although Henry is reported to have converted to Catholicism to preserve the throne, his edict legally recognized the Protestant movement in France.

Zwingli Develops Theocracy

Ulrich Zwingli, a supporter of the Swiss reformation, is of the opinion that a true Christian society should be ruled by two God-ordained officers; the magistrate and the pastor. His patriotism towards the Swiss nation has enabled Zwingli to work for the unification of Zurich's Christian society. Zwingli teaches that both spiritual and secular power is established by God for the realization of God's plan for the world. Rather than set up clergy as secular rulers, Zwingli advocates a sharing of secular power and wealth between religious and state officials.

Calvin Defends Reformation Teachings

John Calvin is attempting to build a more visible "City of God" with Geneva as his starting point. Calvin is famous for systematizing Protestant doctrine and beginning the reform movement in Switzerland, independent of the movement in Germany.

Calvinism resembles Lutheranism in its basic tenants; however, Calvin stresses a doctrine of predestination. He believes that regardless of an individuals actions, their fate had already been determined. That is, some are born for heaven, some are born for hell, and nothing can be done to change that fact. Calvin's reformed church celebrate only the sacraments of Baptism and Communion. He believes that the Church is supreme and must not be restricted by the State.

Battle of Kappel Halts Swiss Reform

Huldreich (Ulrich) Zwingli, peoples' priest at Great Minister in Zurich, was killed today in the Battle of Kappel. Zwingli, best known for his development of evangelical beliefs, died while defending the city of Zurich against the Five Catholic Forest Cantons of Switzerland who were raging battle at the bidding of the German princes.

Zwingli leaves a widow, Anna Meyer, and four children. Funeral services will be handled by the family.

Dear Erasmus

Dear Erasmus,

I am in distress over all of the recent breaks with the Church. I do indeed see the need for reform, but it should come from within the Church rather than from outside it. Can anything be done to stop the attacks on the one true faith?
Brokenhearted

Dear Brokenhearted,

I agree completely. There is a definite need to return to the spirit of the Gospel and traditions of the patriotic Church. The ignorance of the clergy is appalling. Pray for unity.
Erasmus

The Swiss Reformation

Directions: Use the information in the *Swiss Herald News* to answer the following questions.

1. Name three theologians who participated in the Swiss reform.

2. What are the three branches of Calvinism?

3. Describe how the reform movement was received in Switzerland and in France.

4. What is anabaptism? How did the Catholic and Protestant churches treat anabaptism?

5. Summarize Zwingli's theocracy.

6. What is predestination? Who taught it?

King Henry VIII and His Legacy

Directions: Read the following information about the development of the Church of England.

Within one month of each other in 1535, Bishop John Fisher and Sir Thomas More were beheaded in London. Their severed heads were displayed publicly as a warning to others. The person who signed their death warrants was King Henry VIII. The reason was a familiar one—the clash of a king's power versus the Church's.

Henry came to the throne in 1509 following the death of his older brother Arthur, who would have been King. Henry's bride, Catherine of Aragon, had been married to Arthur only a few months before his death. A dispensation given by Pope Julius II allowed Henry to marry his brother's widow, a woman several years older than he.

Henry did not love Catherine; it was also unfortunate that she bore him no male heirs. Their only surviving child was a daughter, Mary. Fearing that the Tudor family's rule would come to an end, by 1527 Henry had convinced himself that God was punishing him for his marriage to Catherine and that a divorce was justified. He had also fallen in love with a young lady at court, Anne Boleyn. He applied to Rome for a divorce from Catherine.

Pope Clement VII faced two dilemmas: first, his immediate predecessor had already given Henry a dispensation; second, Rome was under the control of Emperor Charles V, Catherine of Aragon's uncle. Henry's request was denied.

Henry then appointed one of his supporters, Thomas Cranmer, as Archbishop of Canterbury; Cranmer granted the divorce, and Henry married Anne. Next he railroaded Parliament into passing the Act of Succession (making Anne legitimate queen) and the Act of Supremacy (declaring Henry head of the Church in England).

Henry's friend, Thomas More, quietly resigned as chancellor because of the King's divorce and remarriage. Henry demanded that More take an oath to uphold the Act of Supremacy. When More refused, he was put on trial, found guilty of treason, and beheaded. For a similar reason, John Fisher was also killed.

Ironically, Anne Boleyn also was eventually beheaded. She bore Henry only a daughter (Elizabeth) and was accused of adultery when she fell out of favor with the King.

In all, Henry had six wives. He eventually had a son, Edward, who died at age fifteen.

> *Division has done more to hide Christ from the view of men than all the infidelity that has ever been spoken.*
>
> —George MacDonald

Henry, in his search for political power and personal pleasure, was responsible for England's breaking away from the Church of Rome. Bishop John Fisher and Sir Thomas More both became saints of the Catholic Church.

King Edward VI
(1545–1553)

After Henry's death, his son by Jane Seymour became Edward VI at nine years of age. Since he was too young to reign, the administration of the kingdom fell to his protector, the Archbishop of Canterbury. Cranmer had sanctioned the divorce between Henry VIII and Catherine and blessed the King's union to Anne Boleyn. He now served to lead England into Protestantism. Cranmer, corresponding with Calvin, set up a theological commission that produced a religious blueprint for the Church of England. He translated Luther's catechism into English and authorized the distribution of *Homilies*. In 1549, the *Book of Common Prayer* produced a new English liturgy which was more like a communion service than a Mass, more Lutheran than Catholic. With young Edward's premature death in 1553, Cranmer's influence diminished.

Queen Mary I
(1553–1558)

Mary Tudor, the daughter of Catherine of Aragon and Henry VIII, reigned as queen from 1553–1558. Raised by her Spanish mother as a devout Catholic, Mary I attempted a restoration of Catholicism in England. She sent the Protestant archbishop, Cranmer, to the London Tower. He was replaced by her cousin and influential advisor, Cardinal Reginald Pole. Pole opened the second session of the Council of Trent in 1553 with a call for Church renewal following the principles of humanism. As Archbishop of Canterbury, he called a national synod of bishops in 1555 to initiate reforms in the English Catholic Church. A Catholic revival ensued. As a sign that Protestant tendencies would not be tolerated, Mary I enacted through Parliament the annulment of all laws made under her father and half-brother which separated the English people from the Roman Church. Cranmer was burned at the stake. This set off a persecution of Protestant reformers in England that was to earn the queen the nickname, "Bloody Mary." Her short reign ended in both her death and that of Archbishop Pole.

Queen Elizabeth
(1558–1603)

This daughter of Henry VIII and Anne Boleyn became ruler of England in 1558. During the next forty-five years, this Renaissance queen was to enact reforms which unified England. England prospered under the age of Elizabeth: Catholics did not. (Notable persons during this time included Drake, Raleigh, and Shakespeare.) In 1559, a new Act of Supremacy reestablished the power of the crown. Under Elizabeth, the Church of England (Anglican Church) flourished. Ultimately concerned for political and social stability, Elizabeth desired to see England united. She attempted a compromise between Catholic and Protestant beliefs. Heresy and treason were the same during her reign. Those martyred for religious reasons were convicted in civil court for crimes against the state. In 1570 she was excommunicated by the pope. Afterwards, political rivalry with Catholic France and Spain, more than religious doctrine, separated the English from the Roman Church.

Results of English Reform

In the years between Henry VIII and Elizabeth I, the English reform movement emerged as an independent religious group. The times were confusing and bloody, marked with flip-flopping doctrinal positions and persecutions. England developed a religious form which was neither Catholic nor Protestant, but English. Following is a summary of Anglican belief:

- The pope does not have universal authority over the whole Church.

- The English crown (reigning king or queen) is head of the Church in England.

- There are seven sacraments, including priesthood with optional celibacy. (The English Church retained most Catholic doctrines and practices.)

Worship was to be celebrated in English following the rituals found in the *Book of Common Prayer*.

150

Rulers

Part A

Directions: In each of the boxes, identify persons who were contemporaries of these English rulers and who assisted or opposed them.

Henry VIII	Edward VI

Mary I	Elizabeth I

151

Part B

Directions: Compare Thomas More with Thomas Becket. Give at least three similarities and three differences.

The Council of Trent

Directions: Read the following information about the Council of Trent.

When the first session of the council convened to order under Pope Paul III on December 3, 1545, the Council fathers faced a two-fold task: the treatment of Catholic belief in opposition to the new theologies of the Protestants and the reformation of Catholic life. They met at Trent, a small town in Northern Italy. When it concluded, the council consisted of three sessions over a period of nearly twenty years (1545–1563).

Protestant groups had two things in common; they rejected the authority of the pope and based their theologies on the authority of Scripture alone. In reaction to this position, the Tridentine fathers identified three sources for Catholic positions: the Bible, teachings of the Fathers of the Church, and decrees of former councils and popes. This triple source of authority is known as Catholic Tradition. Furthermore, the positions taken at Trent were based on a consensus of the popes, cardinals, bishops, theologians, and canonists (church lawyers), whereas most of the positions held by the Protestant religions resulted from one reformer's teachings. The reformed Catholic positions, therefore, resulted from a unity between Catholic theologians and the hierarchy (leadership) of the Church. There was no basic theological unity between the various Protestant groups, whose ideas were reactions to the preexistent beliefs and practices of the Catholic Church. Thus, the Council of Trent was not merely a reaction to reformers, but a serious comprehensive renewal of the Church founded by Jesus Christ and developing out of the apostolic community of Jerusalem.

As the council fathers went about their work, they carefully examined three main areas of religious life: doctrinal statements, disciplinary practices, and the sacraments. Since Luther and others attacked the traditions, doctrines, and practices of Catholic life, the Catholic reformers took a long, hard look at everything that pertained to being a good Catholic.

The Council's Decrees

In the first session, the council established its purpose: to express Catholic doctrine as it came to be understood in the long tradition of the Church. The Catholic theologians came prepared. Each of the sixteen decrees (formal written conclusions on specific topics) traced the history of Catholic belief on a particular topic. Attached to the decrees were canons (short statements summarizing exactly what Catholics believed) each concluding with the condemnation *anathema sit*. The messages conveyed through these conciliar decrees were clear: true Catholics believe this doctrine; here is why we believe it; here is the historical development of the belief; anyone who denies it is condemned.

From Luther to Trent

Summary of Trent's Decrees

Directions: Study the information below about the agenda of the Council of Trent.

A. Doctrinal Decrees from the Church

In response to the Protestant reformers, the Council restated key Church doctrines in light of their historical development from the Church's tradition.

1. *Sacred Scripture*—The Council endorsed the Latin Vulgate Bible containing forty-six Old Testament books and decreed that authentic interpretation belongs to the Church.

   . . . Luther accepted thirty-nine books from the Old Testament and believed in private interpretation.

2. *Salvation*—The Council held that we are saved by the grace and merits of Jesus Christ.

   . . . Calvin preached predestination from birth.

3. *Sacraments in General*—Catholics practice seven sacraments.

   . . . Luther, Zwingli, and Calvin found only Baptism and Holy Communion in the Scriptures.

4. *Original Sin*—Adam's sin is passed on through birth; therefore, infants must be baptized.

   . . . Calvin and Anabaptists practiced adult baptism; there is no original sin.

5. *Justification*—Everyone is justified by the grace, justice, and mercy of God, exemplified by good works.

   . . . Luther taught that we are justified by faith alone.

> What are these new doctrines? The gospel? Why, that is 1,522 years old. The teachings of the apostles? Why they are almost as old as the gospel. . . We will try everything by the touchstone of the gospel and the fire of Paul.
>
> —Philip Melanchthon

153

From Luther to Trent

B. Decrees Reforming Church practices

1. Concerning bishops and priests

   . . . *Celibacy was reaffirmed; there were to be no bishop-princes, nor private chaplaincy. A bishop must reside in his diocese, with no multi-dioceses for bishops. Concerning the breviary, the Liturgy of the Hours must be prayed by all clergy daily.*

2. Regulating the collection of Church fees

   . . . *There were to be indulgence/alms collectors; stipends (fees for performing the sacraments) would go to the priest.*

   . . . *A church tax (cathedraticum) was to be assessed annually to each parish in the diocese by the bishop.*

3. Training of clergy

   . . . *Seminaries for the careful training of priests must be set up by all bishops in their dioceses. Priests must be twenty-four-years-old to be ordained and not of illegitimate birth.*

4. Concerning the Index of Forbidden Books

   . . . *All book reformers were condemned and Catholics were forbidden to read them under penalty of excommunication. (Note: The Index was abolished by the Second Vatican Council.)*

5. Regarding a catechism

   . . . *In order to propagate the decrees of Trent, a special religion book was published containing all the teachings of the Council.*

154

C. Decrees on Worship and Sacraments

1. Three decrees on the Holy Eucharist were affirmed:

    . . . *The doctrine of the real presence of Christ present in the Eucharist is emphasized.*

    . . . *Trent reaffirmed transubstantiation, the teaching of Lateran IV (1215) that the bread and wine becomes the real body and blood of Christ at the Consecration of Mass.*

    . . . *The Holy Sacrifice of the crucified Christ is the central theme for Mass.*

2. Tridentine Mass

    . . . *Only Latin could be used at Mass; a new Roman missal with revised Mass was published.*

    . . . *Luther and others used the vernacular in their worship services.*

3. Other Eucharistic practices

    . . . *Communion under both species was forbidden; communion to children was reaffirmed.*

    . . . *Luther and others passed the cup at Communion; Calvin forbade children from receiving communion.*

4. Separate decrees on Baptism, Confirmation, Penance, Extreme Unction, and Holy Orders

    . . . *After reviewing the scriptural, historical, and theological backgrounds to these sacraments, the Council's decrees included theological rationale and detailed procedures for the proper ministration of each sacrament. (Note: The Second Vatican Council did the same in the twentieth century, updating the liturgical practices of each sacrament.)*

5. Devotional Practices

    . . . *The Council authorized the celebration of various devotional practices including those honoring the Blessed Virgin Mary, veneration of the saints, and the use of sacramentals such as the rosary, holy water, statues, and relics.*

Reformation Comparisons

Part A

Directions: Read each of the statements below carefully. Determine which statements would have been made by one of the Protestant reformers (R) and which statement represents a teaching of the Council of Trent (C).

1. _____ Scripture is the only source of faith.

2. _____ There are seven sacraments.

3. _____ Everyone is a priest.

4. _____ People are justified by faith alone.

5. _____ Salvation comes by faith and good works done in cooperation with God's grace.

6. _____ Baptism and Communion are the only true sacraments.

7. _____ From birth we are predestined by God.

8. _____ Faith is based on scripture and sacred tradition.

9. _____ At the Eucharistic celebration, the bread and wine are transubstantially changed into the real presence of Christ.

10. _____ Communion under both species is forbidden, but children may receive communion.

Part B

Directions: Write the correct information on the blank.

1. The Catholic Counter-Reformation took place at Trent which was located in this country._____

2. The years for the Council of Trent were from_____ to_____.

3. The pope who convened the first session of Trent was _____.

4. The task of the Council was_____.

5. The Council fathers attempted to accomplish this through the Council of Trent._____

Part C

Directions: Answer the following questions with complete sentences.

1. What two characteristics did the Protestants have in common?

2. Roman Catholic doctrines developed from three sources of authority known collectively as our tradition. What are the three sources?

   a.

   b.

   c.

3. Which three main areas of religious life did the council fathers carefully examine at Trent? Give examples of each.

   a.

   b.

   c.

4. Explain the significance of the sixteen conciliar decrees.

5. Explain the roles played by theologians, bishops, and popes during the council.

Part D

Directions: Define the following terms, all of which came from the Council of Trent.

1. Cathedraticum

2. Seminary

3. Transubstantiation

4. Breviary

5. Index of Forbidden Books

Part 5

From Modernism to the Modern Era

Go, therefore, and make disciples of all nations, baptizing them in the name of the Father, and of the Son, and of the holy Spirit, teaching them to observe all that I have commanded you. And behold, I am with you always, until the end of the age."

—*Matthew 28:19–20*

The eighteenth and nineteenth centuries were an era of turmoil for the world and for the pilgrim Church. Revolutionary ideas like the humanist movement (revival of classical learning) and the effects of the protestant movement led to the beginning of the enlightenment. The Church was often judged guilty of absolutism. Unbelief, along with ruthless and militaristic nationalism, was widespread. As a result, Europe lost all semblance of political and spiritual unity.

The kings and emperors of Christian Europe began to fall victim to the new democratic form of nationalism. By the eighteenth century, the politics of Europe dictated that the religion of the ruler was also the religion of the people. Monarchies oppressed religion whenever it seemed to divide the loyalties of the people. In practice, rulers viewed the pope as another king, and a foreign one at that. With the French Revolution and the rise of Napoleon, a new age began in Europe. Everywhere that the citizen-emperor's troops went, they took with them ideas of revolution. Throughout Europe, liberalism fanned protestant hatred for Catholicism. The new nationalistic governments of Europe forced the papacy to reconsider its position and authority as a political entity.

The twentieth century brought a new set of challenges. How would the Church adapt itself to the modern era without compromising the counter-cultural teachings of Jesus that are its foundation? Remaining a forthful disciple in the present day necessitates relying on the guidance of the Holy Spirit and renewing our dedication to the teachings of the Scriptures and the Church Fathers.

Liberty! Equality! Fraternity!

Directions: Read the following description of the Church's situation during the nineteenth century.

In the nineteenth century, new ideas of liberty, equality, and fraternity became a way of life in modern civilization. In 1864, Pope Pius IX condemned these and the revolutionary movements they represented in the writing, "Syllabus of Errors." In the nineteenth century, these had become identified with certain philosophies, heresies, and secular movements that were non-Christian and anti-Catholic, according to Pope Pius IX. Darwinism, evolution, communism, socialism, Marxism and many other contemporary movements (eighty in all) were condemned in the "Syllabus."

a. Secular Philosophies

The enlightenment challenged people to put their confidence in human reason and their faith in nature. It applied the scientific method (independent inquiry and knowledge derived from observable data) to human self-understanding. German philosopher Immanuel Kant (1724–1804), put the challenge simply: "Dare to Know! Have the courage to use your own intelligence." The British empiricist, David Hume proclaimed, " It is impossible to prove from data of the senses, the existence of a soul." Other philosophers such as Descartes, Spinoza, Leibnitz, Locke, and Montesquieu also taught that people should put faith in human nature and the world. These radical philosophers prized freedom and liberty as the greatest human values. They ridiculed Catholic doctrines, calling Catholicism "a religion of magic and marble."

The enlightenment created a new "religion" called deism. It viewed God as an impersonal, detached, cosmic watchmaker. The philosophers of enlightenment taught that God created the world with its own internal natural laws and after that just sat back and watched it tick. Human beings are left on their own because the deist's God doesn't interfere in human affairs. Many of the American revolutionaries were deists, including Benjamin Franklin, Thomas Jefferson, and some of the signers of the Declaration of Independence. In France, Voltaire, the main deist, led the attack against Christianity and all organized religion. The rapidly growing Freemason movement in Europe looked to deism as the main religion.

We come to know truth not only by reason, but still more so through our hearts.

—Blaise Pascal

161

From Modernism to the Modern Era

b. Godless Political Philosophies

1. **Absolutism:** King Louis XIV, the Sun-King of France, considered himself next to God. He promoted a political philosophy of absolute power by divine right. Since God gave him the position of monarch of France, he had the right to rule as he saw fit—with no outside interference, even from the pope. *The Four Articles* of 1682 rejected papal authority. They included such ideas as

   a.) The Church and pope have no power over monarchs.

   b.) The authority of a general or national council is greater than that of a pope.

   c.) The primacy of the pope must be exercised with consideration for the customs of the local Church.

   d.) Decrees of a pope on matters of faith are not binding until the whole Church consents to them.

   King Louis forced the clergy to accept these ideas. He went so far as to demand that French seminaries teach these ideas to aspiring clergy.

2. **Gallicanism:** King Louis XIV rejected the central authority of papal power over the whole Church. His ideas created a national spirit called Gallicanism, which was critical of the Church. This spirit produced a religious nationalism that emphasized freedom from the power of the Church over national affairs. All teaching, including theology, was considered the province of Gallicanism.

   French people who supported the pope and rejected Gallicanism were called *ultramontanes* (across the mountains). These people continued to seek guidance from the Church across the Alps—in Rome. French Jesuits were among the *ultramontanes*. Tied closely to the aristocracy as tutors of families of nobility, the Jesuits were religious conservatives; however, they were very liberal in their personal affairs. In 1773, under pressure of King Louis XV, the Jesuits worldwide were suppressed by Pope Clement XIV and their order nearly disbanded.

3. **Liberalism:** The "enlightened" thoughts which flowed from the pen of Voltaire were popularized by his successor Jean-Jacques Rousseau. Expanded liberalism called for equality and fraternity in the French nation. The populace turned Gallican ideals which had evolved from an absolutist king into a democratic belief stressing individual liberty. In the heart of the revolution (1793–1795), Christianity was replaced temporarily by a religion of reason. In 1793, an actress-dancer paraded into Notre Dame cathedral and presided over an orgy. The revolutionary leader Robespierre substituted the "God of Reason" for the Christian God. His

162

dictatorial leadership led to a beheading—his own—during the Reign of Terror. By 1801, Church-State relations between France and Rome settled to a point that Napoleon signed a Concordat with Rome, allowing the pope to invest new bishops and people to practice Catholicism, although not as a state religion. The liberalism, equality, and fraternity which had unleashed the French Revolution ushered in a new age of liberalism, progress, and modern civilization.

4. **Indifferentism:** After the Napoleonic period (1801–1815), Church-State relations in Europe stabilized even though the concepts of liberalism continued in secular society. Across the sea, the United States demonstrated that the Church could survive in a liberal social order based on democracy and freedom. In France, ultramontanes led a religious revival between 1817 and 1870. Abbe Lamennais, in 1830, published a little journal advocating complete freedom of conscience, worship, opinion, and popular election. This concept known as indifferentism was condemned by a papal encyclical. Lamennais severed his relationship with the Church and died in poverty.

c. *Career of Pope Pius IX*

When the college of cardinals elected Giovanni-Maria Mastai-Ferretti as Pope Pius IX, they had no idea that this fifty-four-year-old would be the longest reigning pope in history. Europe was ablaze with revolutionary spirit and the influence of political philosophies and movements of the age. Within the Church itself could be found two camps, the conservative ultramontanes and the progressive liberal element. The northern and southern city-states of Italy used political alliances to unify a new republic of Italy. However, the central part of Italy was still the sovereignty of the pope, who used his influence to maintain the rich Papal States. This was the state of affairs as Pope Pius IX, known as Pio Nono ("grandfather"), began his career in papal office. The following dates are significant:

1846 Pope Pius IX was elected.

1847 Pope Pius IX exercised the concept of liberal politics within the Papal States by granting limited power to the people.

1849–1850 The pope was exiled from Rome for eighteen months as Rome set up a republic freed from the temporal powers of the pope.

*Tradition;
I am
tradition.*

—*Pope
Pius IX*

1854 After corresponding with his bishops, Pius IX declared the doctrine of the Immaculate Conception of Mary. (In 1858, the Blessed Virgin appeared to St. Bernadette Soubirous at Lourdes, France, identifying herself as "I am the Immaculate Conception.")

1860 The papal armies were defeated by the Piedmont republican movement. The Papal States were lost. Confined to the Vatican, the pope introduced *L'Oservatore Romano*, the Vatican newspaper, to communicate with the outside world. Pius IX created hundreds of new diocese and bishops all over the world. He instituted *ad limina* visits. (Each bishop must come to the Vatican to report personally the state of his diocese to the pope every five years.) Pius IX began regular public and private audiences with common people.

1864 The encyclical, *Quanta Cura* was published, including the Syllabus of Errors. Pius IX condemned eighty influences on modern society to conserve traditional Catholic belief.

1869–1870 Vatican Council convened and declared the doctrine of papal infallibility after a clash between conservative and liberal elements in the Church.

1871 A new nationalistic Italian republic was established, putting a permanent end to the Papal States. The pope was offered sovereignty over the Vatican, Lateran, and Castel Gandolfo, in addition to a payment of three million Italian lire per year.

1878 Pope Pius IX, "creator of the modern papacy," died at the age of eighty-seven.

The Errors of the Age

Directions: In the *Syllabus of Errors*, Pope Pius IX condemned errors in the following modern philosophies:

a. Enlightenment
b. Deism
c. Indifferentism
d. Gallicanism
e. Liberalism

Determine which condemned belief is described in each of the following statements.

1. ___ The Roman pontiff can and ought to reconcile and harmonize himself with progress, with liberalism, and with modern civilization.

2. ___ It does not pertain exclusively to ecclesiastical jurisdiction to direct the teaching of theology.

3. ___ There exists no supreme all-wise and provident being distinct from this universe; God is the same as the nature of things, and therefore liable to change; and God is really made both in humanity and in the world, and all things are God and have the self-same substance of God; God is one and the same thing with the world, and therefore spirit is the same thing with matter, necessity with liberty, truth with falsehood, good with evil and just with unjust.

4. ___ Bishops ought not, without the permission of the government, to publish even apostolic letters.

5. ___ The prophecies and miracles recorded and narrated in Scripture are poetical fictions, and the mysteries of Christian faith a result of philosophical investigations; the books of both Testaments contain mythical inventions; Jesus Christ himself is a mythical fiction.

6. ___ It is false that the civil liberty of all worships and the full power granted to all to openly declare any opinions whatever conduce to corrupt the minds of peoples and propagate the plague of indifferentism.

7. ___ The Church has no power of employing force, nor has it any temporal power, direct or indirect.

8. ___ All action of God on humanity and on the world is denied.

9. ___ All the truths of religion flow from the natural force of human reason; hence reason is the chief rule whereby we can and should obtain the knowledge of all truths of every kind.

10. __ People may in the practice of any religion whatever find the path to eternal salvation.

> *The existence of one God is according to reason; the resurrection of the dead, above reason.*
>
> —John Locke, *An Essay Concerning Human Understanding*

165

Exercise 78

Without the pope there can be no Church, without the Church no Christianity, and without Christianity no religion and no society. . .

—Lamennais

Infallibility

Directions: Read the following explanation of the Church's teachings about infallibility.

What is infallibility?

Infallibility is a gift of the spirit to all the People of God, protecting the Church from errors in matters of faith and morals. It operates in the person who speaks and in the people who listen.

> **Faith**—*something we must believe to be saved.*

> **Morals**—*principles dealing with proper conduct to be saved.*

Who can speak infallibly?

1. The People of God—Collectively

In any truth or moral teaching which the whole Church holds to be true (*e.g.*, the Trinity, the Incarnation)

2. The College of Bishops—United

When, in union with the Holy Father, they teach a doctrine (*e.g.*, Infallibility of the Holy Father)

From Modernism to the Modern Era

3. The Pope—Individually

When the pope proclaims a doctrine of faith or morals, speaking *ex cathedra* as Chief Shepherd of all the faithful (*e.g.*, Assumption of Mary, Immaculate Conception)

Why do we believe in infallibility?

Because Christ promised to be with his Church and that the Holy Spirit would be present (*Matthew 28:20, John 16:7–12*)

167

Infallible or Not?

Directions: Listed below are five different situations. Based on your understanding of infallibility, determine whether or not the statements are infallible.

1. _____ The pope and the bishops declare solemnly that Mary was assumed body and soul into heaven.

2. _____ The pope issues an encyclical on human life.

3. _____ The bishops issue a pastoral letter on the economy.

4. _____ The pope declares that Mary was born without original sin.

5. _____ The pope issues a statement that women can never be priests because the apostles were male.

The Two Feet of a Christian

Directions: Study the relationship between the Church's missions of justice and charity.

Justice

Loving another so much that you work to change structures that violate his or her dignity as a human being.

Deals with the *causes* of problems.

- Consumer activist groups
- Pro-life organizations
- Government lobbying
- Amnesty International
- Sanctuary Movement
- Boycotts
- Education and/or job training
- Preventive medical care

Charity

Acts of kindness and generosity aimed at helping those who are in need.

Deals with the *effects* of problems.

- Food banks
- Clothing drives
- Shut-in visitation
- Donations of money, goods, services
- Welfare
- Missionary work
- Hospice care
- St. Vincent de Paul Society

169

To walk—both are needed!

From Modernism to the Modern Era

Catholic Social Teaching at a Glance

Directions: Read the following summary of the church's teachings about social justice.

Rerum Novarum (On the Condition of Workers, Pope Leo XIII, 1891) People have a right to demand just wages, organize into labor unions, and own private property. The encyclical pointed out the dangers in both socialism and liberal capitalism.

Mater et Magistra (Christianity and Social Progress, Pope John XXIII, 1961) All areas of life are interdependent. The impact of the technological revolution, the rise of the welfare state, and the people's desire to participate in the political process demand that the Church analyze current movements in light of the Gospel teachings of Christ.

Pacem in Terris (Peace on Earth, Pope John XXIII, 1963) In the past, religion often found itself to be the ally of the powerful in unjust situations. The Church must turn its might against oppression and work for world peace.

Gaudiem et Spes (Pastoral Constitution on the Church in the Modern World, Vatican II, 1965) The Church can no longer preserve the current state of affairs in the world. The Church must interact with the modern world to promote human dignity and solidarity.

Populorium Progressio (On the Development of Peoples, Pope Paul VI, 1967) The Church must turn its attention to the causes, not merely the results, of injustice. Wealthy nations have a moral obligation to alleviate poverty and aid developing countries.

Octagesima Adveniens (On the Eightieth Anniversary of *Rerum Novarum*, Pope Paul VI, 1971) The Political sector must get involved to insure the basic economic rights of all people.

Evangelii Nutiandi (On Evangelization in the Modern World, Pope Paul VI, 1975) Failure to accept the social implications of the Gospel is a lack of responsiveness to the Gospel itself, and hence a defect in faith. Faith in the kingdom of God requires action in the life of the believer.

To Live in Christ Jesus (United States Bishops' Pastoral Letter, 1976) Those who have been particularly discriminated against deserve special help. Because of the unique position of the United States in the world, helping the entire human family is an inescapable duty.

Laborem Exercens (On Human Work, Pope John Paul II, 1981)
Workers have rights on the job and in the marketplace.
A spirituality of work places the needs of people over
the production of things.

The Challenge of Peace: God's Promise and Our Response
(United States Bishops' Pastoral Letter, 1983) The proliferation
of nuclear weapons is morally evil. It is morally evil to use
nuclear weapons for counter-population warfare, for the
initiation of a nuclear war, for the conduction of a limited
nuclear war, and for the determent of war on a long-term basis.

Economic Justice for All (United States Bishops' Pastoral Letter,
1986) Every economic decision and institution must be judged
by whether it protects or undermines the dignity of the human
person. All people have a right to participate in the economic
life of society. All members of society have a special obligation
to the poor and vulnerable. Society as a whole, acting through
public and private institutions, has the moral responsibility
to enhance human dignity and protect human rights.

Sollicitudo Res Socialis (On Social Concern, Pope John Paul II, 1987)
The growing gap between the riches of the First World and
the poverty of the Third World calls for a renewed sense of
collaboration for peace and a redirection of resources to
alleviate the suffering of the poor.

Justice Inventory

*No one
is so rich as
not to need
another's
help;*

*no one
so poor as
not to be useful
in some way
to his or her
neighbor.*

172

*And the
disposition to
ask assistance
from others
with
confidence,
and to grant it
with kindness,
is part of
our very
nature.*

*—Pope
Leo XIII*

Directions: What is your opinion about the issues below? Place a checkmark in the column which best describes your viewpoint.

Issue	*Agree*	*Disagree*	*Not Sure*
1. A consistent ethic for human life involves working to protect the lives of the unborn, the elderly, those who are oppressed, and those who are poor.	_____	_____	_____
2. Affirmative action plans are necessary in the business sector to end discrimination.	_____	_____	_____
3. Sometimes, as in the case of offering public sanctuary, human conscience and religious teaching must come before the secular law of the land.	_____	_____	_____
4. Faithfulness to the Gospel requires that we take steps to end materialism.	_____	_____	_____
5. Working to end oppression in foreign countries and establish human rights must come before the national interests of this country.	_____	_____	_____
6. In order to be a good Catholic, I must work for justice.	_____	_____	_____

America's Big Mac Stomach

Directions: The following article appeared in *The Catholic Worker* in 1981. Read it carefully and prepare to share your response.

Did I Tell You I was working at McDonald's? Talk about losing any vestige of recollection! It is always complete chaos. This last weekend down in Tucson I heard Fr. Matthew Fox speak. Intermingled with some good thoughts on creation-centered spirituality, he mentioned some things going on in South America; for instance, razing huge areas of the great rain forest in order to make grazing lands for cattle. Acres of jungle demolished. I wouldn't think that was so bad except none of the poor in Brazil get any of that protein-rich meat. Those thousands of cattle are raised for the gigantic hamburger chains in North America, *i.e.*, McDonald's.

This unsettled me a little, especially when he said: "Think about that the next time you go to McDonald's—and see if you can avoid it." With all that I have been reading on social justice and some of the workshops I have attended, it strikes me as dimly possible that I should be stepping out in some small (extremely small) way.

Global Village

Last night I went to the store to find out my schedule for this coming week. I was arguing against the idea of quitting: because I need the money, because I want to go to school at Gonzaga, want to order some books (as if I read the ones I already have), etc., and what good would it do anyway?

Of course, as with any futile effort in the line of social justice, they say it's like shooting BB's at elephants. What good did Adolfo Perez Esquivel's imprisonment do (1980 Nobel Prize)? How many deaths did Archbishop Romero's death prevent?

But then again, as Matthew Fox pointed out, we don't seem to be living in our own small countries any longer. It does seem closer to reality to speak of a global village. It would be insane to think some obscure girl in some obscure town at one of hundreds of McDonald's store might have any effect by quitting or raise anyone's consciousness (except, perhaps, her own) . . .

Meanwhile, this materialistic young girl is thinking of the money she wouldn't get. This mentality reaches from her to the store owner, to the McDonald's Company President, to the cattle growers in Brazil . . . Nobody lose any money please, one can't go around losing any precious "money."

Furthermore, those huge tropical rain forests are part of the vast interplay of the earth's climate. What would their eventual destruction (to feed America's Big Mac stomach) influence, if anything?

From Modernism to the Modern Era

A Small Step

Is it a "holy" thing, in the most infinite sense of that word, to be even an insignificant link in an insignificant chain that holds all these people (including myself) bound to some materialistic merry-go-round?

There is always the problem of the young single mother feeding four children. She has no choice if McDonald's is the only job available. But I do. I am not dependent on this huge hamburger chain . . . I just want the money.

And instead of throwing frozen fries into the hot grease and taking them out at the sound of the buzzer, I would rather write. I like to write. In fact, all these words seem a little too much for something very simple like working at a fast food joint. I guess I begin to question its surface simplicity and see if there is anything else there.

Back to the original question: Would Jesus work at McDonald's if he were aware of the Brazilian rain forest? (It's a strange connection, isn't it? There should be something closer to home. But isn't this close to home, in some sense?) He certainly wouldn't work "just for the money." He would have some job with creativity in it, something close to the earth, something he could be an artist in . . . like wood. And he says to me, "the pagans of this world run after these things. But as for you, your Father knows what you need." (Maybe that includes college?)

Besides, prayer is the very heart of social justice. McDonald's is continuous chaos—with no chance that its workers have time to think on their own during an eight-hour shift, much less hang on to any vestige of recollection.

So I think this coming Thursday will be my last day. I worked today. The only thing I could think of as they threw the frozen meat on the grill was those people in Brazil. A rather strange, sad feeling came over me. Especially as I watched the other employees going through all the mechanical movements.

It occurred to me that the sad feeling I got was just due to my own difficulties and that it really didn't matter. But I think Jesus was using that emotion to teach me a little something about "global village" concepts and the unity of humankind.

I think the decision is a good one. At least it's a step in the right direction.[1]

[1]Cathy Euler, *The Catholic Worker* (Winona, Minn.: PACE 12 St. Mary's Press, June-July 1981–82), Issue-B.

1. What is your opinion of the author's course of action? Why?

2. What can you do in your own little corner of the world to promote justice?

Vatican II

> Truth calls for the elimination of every trace of racial discrimination, and the consequent recognition of the inviolable principle that all states are by nature equal in dignity.
>
> —Pope John XXIII

Directions: Read the following description of the renewal initiated by Pope John XXIII and Vatican Council II.

In 1958, the Archbishop of Venice, Angelo Guiseppi Roncalli, was elected the 216th pope of the Roman Catholic Church. The road leading to his election had been a long one. He was born in 1881, the third of thirteen children in an Italian peasant family. He served as a sergeant of the medical corp and later as a lieutenant/chaplain in World War I. After the war, he served in the Vatican Diplomatic Corp for nineteen years before assuming his duties as the Archbishop of Venice.

At age seventy-seven he was elected to the papacy as a compromise candidate and became Pope John XXIII. The cardinals viewed his advanced age as a sign that his papacy would be a short one and that he could not possibly make too many changes in the interim. Although his reign lasted only five years, he was able to change the Church more than any other pope of modern times.

One of the first changes he made was to expand the college of cardinals. A four-hundred-year-old tradition limited their number to seventy. By including more members from various nations, he opened the Church to the richness of cultural diversity in the world. He called for the updating of canon law, and he left the Vatican to visit hospitals, parishes, jails, and people on street corners. He hosted dinner parties, told jokes, and spent time with common families. He was known for his quick wit and sense of humor, once remarking: "God knew for seventy years that I would be pope someday; why didn't he make me at least a little photogenic?" He extended a welcome to Jews and Protestants alike and did much to foster a spirit of ecumenism within the Church.

Three months into his pontificate he announced to a group of cardinals that he intended to call a council. He wrote in his diary, "I expected that after hearing what I had to say, they would have crowded around me to express approval and good wishes. Instead there was an unbroken and impressive silence." Despite numerous attempts at stalling by the curia, the Council opened in 1962.

In the past, Church councils were called in times of great crisis. Vatican II was called to promote the unity of all Christians and to study how the Church could adapt itself to the modern world. Important changes were made in five areas of Church life: the liturgy, the Church's understanding of itself, the attitude of the Church toward other Christians, a renewal of the understanding of the Church's place in history, and an increased dialogue with the modern world.

Liturgy: Vatican II brought about a renewal of liturgical ministries. It stressed the nature of the liturgy was more than its sacredness as a means of salvation. The celebrant turned to face the congregation; prayers were recited in the vernacular, the language of the people.

The Church's Understanding of Itself: Vatican II defined the Church as the people of God, who share in the responsibilities of making Christ present in the world today. The collegial nature of the bishops was expressed, as well as the common priesthood of all believers.

The Attitude of the Church toward Other Christians: The Council Fathers encouraged an ecumenical spirit. Respect for the dignity of others and the faith stance of other religious organizations fostered free inquiry and joint study groups.

Understanding the Church's Place in History: The Council Fathers understood that the doctrines of the Church are culturally conditioned. After careful study they attempted to return Church practices to the original vision and intent of the apostles.

The Church's Dialogue with the Modern World: Vatican II began to encourage greater biblical scholarship and new forms of spirituality for the laity. The Church turned its attention to the cause of promoting social justice and began to teach Christians how to be faithful to the message of Jesus Christ in the context of the modern world.

Since many attribute the Second Vatican Council's openness to the inspiration of the Holy Spirit, it is sometimes referred to as "a second Pentecost."

The Council produced sixteen documents of three types:

- Constitutions (authoritative statements dealing with official doctrine or concerned with the Church's care for the world)

- Decrees (legislative enactments)

- Declarations (statements of Church position)

Seven of the documents merit special attention:

Constitution on the Church describes the Church as the people of God, as a sacrament, and as a pilgrim.

The Church in the Modern World describes the Church as a servant to the modern world.

Decree on Ecumenism voices a mandate for all to work for Christian unity.

Constitution on the Sacred Liturgy calls for full participation of the laity in the vernacular.

Constitution on Divine Revelation describes revelation as God's self-disclosure; it encourages Bible study.

Declaration on Religious Freedom guarantees freedom of worship.

Declaration of the Relationship of the Church to Non-Christian Religions ends all forms of religious persecution and condemns religious discrimination.

178

A New Pentecost

Directions: Answer and discuss the following questions.

1. How did the personality of Pope John XXIII contribute to the "open door" policy of Vatican II?

2. How was Vatican II different from preceding councils?

3. What does the term *collegiality* mean?

4. Summarize some of the differences between the pre-Vatican II Church and the Church today.

5. Imagine that the pope has just called for another ecumenical council of bishops (*i.e.*, Vatican III). Where do you think this council would be held? What would be on the agenda? Give reasons for your answers.

Fitting In

Directions: Read the following description of practiced ways to become a more active part of your church.

Being a Catholic means being part of something much bigger than just yourself. Church history is a journey that you are invited to join. You are asked to help form a link with those who have gone before, join with those who are part of the Church now, and forge a link with those who will come after you. Looking back, we see that there have been both good and bad times in the Church's historical pilgrimage. There were times when storm clouds were so thick and Church leadership so poor that some believed the Church would not survive. Now it stands on the threshold of the twenty-first century. The Church looks at you, one of today's pilgrims, and invites you to be part of this spiritual journey through time, affirming Christ yesterday, today, and forever.

Through the Holy Spirit, your task is to bring Jesus into the situations where you find yourself. He needs your hands, feet, eyes, ears, and heart to be there—not because he is weak or unable to do the job by himself—but because he has chosen to operate his plan of salvation by trusting you to make him real and present in the world.

You were created for a role in that plan, and it is a role that only you can fulfill. It may not be one recorded in history books; but whatever your niche, large or small, it is of infinite importance because only you can do it. If you do not do it, then it simply will not get done. Yes, Jesus will still live and act in the world through his Church, but in one small corner he will not be as real to others because someone chose not to bring him there.

All this is not meant to cause guilt or make you fearful of your call to be a Catholic Christian. It is simply to emphasize God's love for you and total trust in you. He chooses, however, to depend on your willingness to respond to him.

Just how do we do this in practical ways? By Baptism, we are all called to a general mission called witnessing. Being a witness does not mean standing on a soap box or being a religious fanatic who discusses religious topics endlessly. Certainly, you may be called upon at times to explain your beliefs to others, even to defend them to hostile questioners; that is an important part of witnessing. But it also means making decisions in your field of work based on Christian principles. If you are a student, it means doing your best with your studies even when they seem boring or standing up for a friend who is being torn to pieces by gossip. If you are an employee, it means giving honest work in exchange for your pay. If you are an employer, it means paying employees a decent wage and respecting their rights and dignity. These are all ways of witnessing through action the belief that Christianity does have relevance to society today. It is our responsibility—and privilege—to be fully Christian witnesses in these circumstances.

Besides a general call to witness because of Baptism, members of today's Church have many opportunities for service depending on their abilities. These are called ministries. In an age when institutions turn some people off, it is important that people make the institutional Church meaningful to today's world.

What are the various means by which the laity can serve in church ministries? One is through participation in liturgical celebrations. For instance, if you find Mass boring, what are you doing to make it less so? Do you take an active part when possible? Many parishes offer youth opportunities to be ushers, choir members, altar servers, liturgy planners, lectors, and Eucharistic ministers. These are all vital ministries because we can be truly Christian in our work only if we have been spiritually fed by the life Christ gives in Eucharist.

Increasingly, the laity are taking more responsibility for the sacramental life of parishes by serving on committees that prepare families for Baptism of their babies, adults for membership through RCIA programs, and couples for marriage.

Besides helping in sacramental areas, there are other ways the laity make the institutional Church relevant to modern society. Many parishes have emergency food supplies or soup kitchens, St. Vincent de Paul societies, groups that give emotional support to people torn by separations caused by divorce or death, day care or baby-sitting for young families, and young adult groups to help combat loneliness common in this age group. Visitation committees welcome new people who have moved into the parish and bring both Eucharist and a cheerful smile to the homebound elderly and sick. Education programs and youth groups are operated by DREs (Directors of Religious Education) and youth ministers.

Further opportunities for service in the Church have developed in part because of the shortage of ordained priest and few people in religious life. Catholic schools are increasingly staffed by lay administrators and lay teachers. Lay people sometimes conduct communion services and wake services at funeral homes. Some parishes have paid lay administrators who take charge of the everyday operation of the parish to free the pastor to serve the spiritual needs of the people. Most parishes also have parish councils in which lay people make decisions about the life of a parish.

The pilgrim Church needs all it is members to be fully functional in today's world. What do you see as your part?

> People
> go forth
> to wonder
> at the
> height of
> mountains,
> the huge
> waves of the
> sea, the
> broad flow
> of rivers,
> the extent
> of the ocean,
> the course
> of the
> stars—and
> forget to
> wonder at
> themselves.
>
> —St. Augustine

182

Ministry Survey

Directions: Use the following activities to reflect on your role as a minister.

1. In which of the following ways would you be comfortable as a witness?

   _____ Refusing to allow someone else to copy your homework

   _____ Comforting a friend who just got eliminated from the basketball team

   _____ Continuing to clean the frier at the fast-food place where you work while other workers stand around talking

   _____ Explaining to a Protestant friend why Catholics believe in honoring the saints

   _____ Admitting you are a Catholic to someone who just made fun of Mass

2. Which ways of witnessing are hardest for you? What can you do to be a more effective witness?

3. Put an X on the line next to the words and phrases that describe you.

   ___ patient

   ___ intelligent

   ___ like children

   ___ sensitive to others' feelings

   ___ good organizer

   ___ speak well

   ___ fun-loving

   ___ extroverted

   ___ introverted

   ___ good listener

   ___ dependable

   ___ like to learn new things

   ___ enthusiastic

   ___ see more to people than just physical attractiveness

   ___ good at sports

   ___ easy-going

   ___ think before making decisions

   ___ take a relationship with God seriously

   ___ other

4. Using the list above, write a statement describing yourself.

5. Which of the following ministries would you feel comfortable participating in now? Mark them with an X. Which would you consider sometime later in life? Mark them with an L.

____ Choir member

____ Liturgy planner

____ Lector

____ Eucharistic minister

____ Preparation program for infant baptism

____ RCIA program for adult baptism preparation

____ Marriage preparation program

____ Helping at a soup kitchen

____ Usher

____ Altar server

____ Belonging to St. Vincent de Paul society

____ Serving on Parish council

____ Being a parish administrator

____ Setting up support group for those who are grieving

____ Setting up support group for those who are divorced

____ Baby-sitting during a parish program

____ Visitation committee

____ Parish religious education program

____ Belonging to youth group

____ Becoming a teacher in a religious school

____ Leading a Scripture service at a Funeral home

____ Other: _____
_____

183

6. How do you think God lets people know what he wants them to do with their lives?

Gospel-Based Spirituality

> We
> think
> our life is
> important
> to ourselves
> alone,
> and do not
> know that
> our life is
> more
> important
> to the
> Living God
> than it is to
> our own
> selves.
>
> —Thomas Merton

184

Directions: Catholicism is based on the teachings of Jesus Christ. In essence we are *called* individually to follow God's ways. We are *commissioned* to continue the ministry of Jesus Christ. We are asked to *await the final coming* of Christ at the end of time. Read and reflect on the Scripture passages listed below, then answer the questions.

A. **The Call**
   John 1:35–51
   Mark 6:30–33

   Do you recognize Jesus Christ as your Lord and Savior? How do you answer his call to you? Is your commitment to Jesus Christ grounded in prayer? Explain your answers.

B. The Commission

Luke 10:1–9
Luke 9:57–62
Luke 12:2–9

How do your actions show your commitment to Jesus Christ? Do you procrastinate instead of getting involved? Do you have the courage to stand up for your religious convictions? Explain your answers.

185

C. Waiting for the Lord
Luke 22:14–20

Do you draw strength and sustenance for the Christian life from Eucharist? Do you allow Eucharist to transform you into an agent for the kingdom of God? Explain your answers.

186

Peak Moments

Directions: In "Ten 'Peak Moments' of Church History," Rev. Alfred McBride lists three criteria for determining the historical significance of events in Church history.

    a.   The event must advance the Church's mission and ministry in a significant way.

    b.   It must promote a growth-filled and vibrant faith in Jesus Christ.

    c.   It must still affect the Church today.[1]

Use McBride's criteria to determine your own list of top ten events. For each event, describe what happened and give specific evidence that it meets the three criteria. The first event, Pentecost, provides an example. Choose nine more.

1. *Pentecost: The Holy Spirit comes to the apostles,*

    a.   *The gift of the Holy Spirit sanctified the Church forever. The Spirit enabled all believers to come to God through Jesus Christ.*

    b.   *The Spirit enabled the apostles to proclaim boldly the death and resurrection of Jesus Christ. Thousands converted to Christianity because of their preaching.*

    c.   *The Church began on the feast of Pentecost. Without the Spirit, no Church would exist today.*

2. Event:

    a.

    b.

    c.

> *Of the past, nothing should remain but sorrow for sin; of the future, nothing anticipated but the hope of heaven; of the present, one sole and only aim to fulfill in every moment God's adorable will.*
>
> —St. Elizabeth Ann Seton

187

[1] Alfred McBride, O. Praem, "Ten 'Peak Moments' of Church History," *Catholic Update.* (Cincinnati: St. Anthony Messenger Press, 1987.)

From Modernism to the Modern Era

3. Event:

   a.

   b.

   c.

4. Event:

   a.

   b.

   c.

5. Event:

   a.

   b.

   c.

6. Event:

   a.

   b.

   c.

188

7. Event:

    a.

    b.

    c.

8. Event:

    a.

    b.

    c.

9. Event:

    a.

    b.

    c.

189

10. Event:

    a.

    b.

    c.

Which Model Fits Best?

Directions: Record your list of the top ten events of Church history. Then review the information in **Exercise 1**, Models of the Church. Determine which model of the Church is best exemplified by each event and cite reasons for your answer. Pentecost provides an example.

1. Event: *Pentecost*

   Model: *Church as Herald*

   Reason: *The apostles' preaching at Pentecost introduced people to the Good News of Jesus' death and resurrection.*

2. Event:

   Model:

   Reason:

3. Event

   Model:

   Reason:

4. Event:

   Model:

   Reason:

5. Event:

   Model:

   Reason:

The influence of Christianity has mounted and has never been greater than it is today.

—Kenneth Latourette

From Modernism to the Modern Era

6. Event:

   Model:

   Reason:

7. Event:

   Model:

   Reason:

8. Event:

   Model:

   Reason:

9. Event:

   Model:

   Reason:

10. Event:

    Model:

    Reason:

Acknowledgments

For permission to reprint all works in this volume, grateful acknowledgment is made to the following holders of copyright, publisher, or representatives.

Lesson 8, 23; Handout 16, 52

Excerpts from *Eerdman's Handbook to the History of Christianity* by Dr. Tim Dowley. Copyright © 1977, Lion Publishing, Oxford, England.

Lesson 14, Handout 28

Excerpt from *Readings in Church History*, edited by Colman J. Garry, OSB. Copyright © 1985. Used with permission of Tabor Publishing, Allen, TX.

Lesson 14, Handout 28

Excerpt from *The Early Christians* by Eberhard Arnold, copyright 1972. Reprinted with permission from Plough Publishing House, Farmington, PA.

Lesson 14, Handout 28

Excerpt from *A New Eusebius* edited by J. Stevenson. Copyright © 1957, Holy Trinity Church, London, England. Used by permission of the publishers.

THE PUBLISHER

All instructional materials identified by the TAP® (Teachers/Authors/Publishers) trademark are developed by a national network of teachers whose collective educational experience distinguishes the publishing objective of The Center for Learning, a non-profit educational corporation founded in 1970.

Concentrating on values-related disciplines, The Center publishes humanities and religion curriculum units for use in public and private schools and other educational settings. Approximately 300 language arts, social studies, novel/drama, life issues, and faith publications are available.

While acutely aware of the challenges and uncertain solutions to growing educational problems, The Center is committed to quality curriculum development and to the expansion of learning opportunities for all students. Publications are regularly evaluated and updated to meet the changing and diverse needs of teachers and students. Teachers may offer suggestions for development of new publications or revisions of existing titles by contacting

The Center for Learning

Administrative/Editorial Office
21590 Center Ridge Road
Rocky River, Ohio, 44116
(216) 331-1404 • FAX (216) 331-5414

For a free catalog, containing order and price information, and a descriptive listing of titles, contact

The Center for Learning

Shipping/Business Office
P.O. Box 910
Villa Maria, PA 16155
(412) 964-8083 • (800) 767-9090
FAX (412) 964-8992